Rudolf Steiner

Lectures and Courses on
Christian-religious Work
IV

The Essence of
the Active Word

Four lectures with answers to questions,
held in Stuttgart, Germany
from July 11 to 14, 1923

With documentary additions

ANTHROPOSOPHICAL PUBLICATIONS
FREMONT, MICHIGAN USA

The Essence of the Active Word
Copyright © 2024 by
Anthroposophical Publications
https://AnthroposophicalPublications.org/

All rights reserved. No part of this book may be reproduced in any form or by any electronic or mechanical means including information storage and retrieval systems, without permission in writing from the author. The only exception is by a reviewer, who may quote short excerpts in a review.GA# 345.

Translation of Lectures by
Hanna von Maltitz

Translation of other material by
James D. Stewart

Cover painting, "Twin Souls"
by Hanna von Maltitz
https://go.elib.com/TwinSouls

Thanks to the *Basil Gibaud Memorial Trust*
for their support in the creation of this translation.

Cover designed by James D. Stewart

Rudolf Steiner Portrait by
Peter Gospodinov

The e.Lib, Inc.
Visit the website at https://www.elib.com/

Printed in the United States of America

First Printing: June 2024

ISBN-13: 978-1-948302-63-0 paperback
978-1-948302-62-3 eBook

Table of Contents

ABOUT THE PUBLICATION OF LECTURES BY RUDOLF STEINER VII
SUMMARIES OF LECTURES IX
ABOUT THIS EDITION XI
TRANSLATOR'S NOTE XIII
FIRST LECTURE 1
SECOND LECTURE 15
THIRD LECTURE 35
FOURTH LECTURE 51
DIRECTORY OF RUDOLF STEINER'S ORIGINAL MANUSCRIPTS 61
  JOHN 17, 1-9: AFTER JESUS HAD SPOKEN 63
  EPISTLES: 65
    Advent.. 65
    Christmas... 71
    Epiphany.. 77
    Passion Week, Holy Week, Easter............ 81
    Ascension and Pentecost 92
    St. John's Tide 100
    Michaelmas... 103
  CHILDREN'S FUNERAL 107
  ACT OF CONSECRATION OF THE DEAD 115
  WEDDING CEREMONY 116
NOTES.. 123
REGISTER OF NAMES 127
APPENDIX I 129
  SPEECH AT THE CREMATION OF HERMANN LINDE. 129

APPENDIX II 139
   A NOTE FROM GA 342 139
ABOUT THE LECTURER 145
ABOUT THE TRANSLATOR......................... 147
ON-LINE RESOURCES 149
OTHER BOOKS 151

About the publication of Lectures by Rudolf Steiner

The complete works of Rudolf Steiner (1861-1925) is divided into three parts: the written works, lectures and artistic work.

From 1900 to 1924 the open lectures, courses as well as lectures to members of the Theosophical and later of the Anthroposophical Society, Rudolf Steiner did not originally want to have written down because "the spoken word brings across something specific". Later, due to incomplete and error filled auditory reports having been customised and spread, he was prompted to regulate the notes taken. This task he gave Marie Steiner-von Sivers. She was incumbent with the stenographers, the management of transcripts and the publication of the need for issuing a review of the texts. As Rudolf Steiner, due to a shortage of time, could only in rare cases correct the transcripts himself, it must be taken into account that all open lectures must be considered with reservations: "It must be realized that in anything I have not reviewed there might be some errors."

Regarding the relationship of lectures to the members which are only available internally in printed manuscripts, Rudolf Steiner expressed himself in "[The Story of My Life](#)" (Chapter 35). The corresponding text is given at the end of this publication. What is said there is equally valid to single fields of knowledge which borders on the basics of spiritual science directed at loyal participants.

After the death of Marie Steiner (1867-1948) her guidelines were adhered to in creating the publication of the *Complete Works* (Gesamtausgabe). This particular publication forms a part of this Complete Works. If necessary, you will find further information on text documents at the beginning of the Notes.

Summaries Of Lectures

Lecture I   July 11, 1923

The development of the work of The Christian Community from its inception. • Symptoms of the undercurrents in spiritual streams at the present time. • Regarding Ahrimanic forces absorbed by humanity through outer culture and making it harmless. • Answers to questions from the audience. • The right way of being immersed in the ritual. • The ritual as the speech of the higher world. • Daily self-participation with the Act of Consecration of Man. • Permeating the self with priest consciousness.

Lecture II   July 12, 1923

Difficulties in the viewpoints of the relationships of the Movement for Religious Renewal and the Anthroposophical Movement. • Inner truth is necessary as opposed to the unconscious untruthfulness of today. • The necessity for an intention in the search of knowledge towards making the spiritual valid again within the nature of knowledge. • The relationship of mankind to the ritual. • Answers to questions from the participants.

Lecture III   July 13, 1923

Impulses towards sensing oneself in the spiritual world. • The weaving of the genius of speech. • Our relationship to speech. • The word "human" / individual ("Mensch"). • A threefold meditation about "the Being whom I want to describe by the word 'human'". • Experiencing truth in words. • The Priest as genius of speech.

Lecture IV   July 14, 1923

The New Testament as a supersensible revelation. • Regarding the translation of the Gospels. • An example of a new kind of translation: John's Gospel 17, 1-19. • Facts of the spiritual evolution of humanity; • After the Mystery of Golgotha, the consciousness of God penetrated humanity in a different way than previously.

About This Edition

This volume in the series "Lectures and Courses regarding the Christian Religious work" is divided into two sections. The first section includes four lectures, given by Rudolf Steiner in July 1923 to the priests of the "Christian Community," which had been founded ten months earlier in Stuttgart.

In the second section are the original handwritten notes of Rudolf Steiner (slightly reduced). They deal with additions to the wording for rituals already presented in the second and third courses. The originals of these handwritten notes can be found in the Archives of the Rudolf Steiner Estate Administration.

Translator's Note

Dear Reader, I wish you could experience the content of these lectures as a listener, for that was the way in which they were presented. Please imagine Rudolf Steiner speaking to you in these lectures rather than finding hiccups in some of his long sentences. Difficulties abound for a translator in finding just one pesky word to convey the richness of German composite words, but trying to offer the reader a string of alternate words which might fit, could be utterly confusing.

Hanna von Maltitz.
November 2017.

First Lecture

Stuttgart, 11 July 1923

The hearty words just spoken (by Dr Rittelmeyer) are an introduction of the strong impetus towards the founding of this religious community-building and the essentials which will flow through this religious working community depend upon the earnestness, I could say a deepening earnestness, which lay originally in the intention and gave the impetus towards the founding of this religious community movement. It has to be said that during the course of these years there has been within the religious community a continuation of this earnestness and that one can already say, in a certain sense, that the original intention has been proven time and again.

In this movement it also appears clearly that the outer impressions of the rituals — I mean this in the noblest sense of the word — work right into our combined spiritual movement. A strong current working from within, truly intended and also truly coming out in a devotional attitude as we recently had in one of our oldest members of our anthroposophical movement, Herman Linde, being led to his cremation. The impressions which came out, just on this occasion, of the ritual act completely shows that the real intention is well on its way to becoming a reality and can be spoken about in the most varied areas not mentioned until now.

I even have the feeling that the objective and progressing striving of this religious community has gone faster than the inner satisfaction and internal harmonizing in the souls of the individual carriers of these religious thoughts. Things are going well. You can feel yourself drawn out by the way these good things are developing, on the one side, and on the other side you battle with inner soul difficulties with particular meaning, because just at this gathering such inner soul difficulties can be talked about because this particular initial gathering can serve to make the difficulties you have, valid, so we can try during the next days to bring about some harmonizing of these inner difficulties.

It is completely understandable that these inner difficulties are there, because you must, while you are the representatives of the most important spiritual initiative, forever remind yourself that realities in the spiritual world work in a powerful way. Even when you are not aware of them, these realities are there. Events taking place on the surface develop roots especially when it happens in the spiritual sphere when related to good or evil. You must always be aware that if you want to work in the present in a religious area that religious orientated spiritual or non-spiritual streams develop an exceptional activity just at that moment.

Just as we are speaking about this at the moment, there is for example a gathering happening of representatives of the Roman Catholic church in a specific place in Europe, which will probably have a particularly important outcome; at least a remarkable result is being envisaged. Today in fact there are more people than one suspects whose hearts feel deserted by religion. Hearts feel deserted by religion while all too seldom words spoken to them come directly out of the spiritual realm. For quite large layers of humanity, it is simply impossible to address these deserted feelings in their hearts, when it is not addressed in words which are not merely of earthly origin, which implies words presented in a supersensible language in the rituals. You must never forget how powerfully effective the Roman Catholic Church in its mass is just at present, still in its old form yet working strongly on the soul and even more effectively in the way it can be spoken.

One must always be clear about how many powers inherent

First Lecture

in humanity are such that errors are able to enter on this side. Consider, when you ask about circulated poetry of Central Europe today, in circles which usually discuss historical progress, and you will not once have a name mentioned such as "Thirteen Linden" von Weber, who has experienced surprisingly many conditions. Why is this so? Out of what basis, when the work of the Roman Catholic spirit is permeated ... (gap in stenographer notes).

These facts are the outer symptoms for a strong spiritual steam, particularly the Roman Catholic one, which works outwardly. This is quite clear to see. Don't forget these forces stream right through the human soul and also go through your souls and some of you probably ascribe it to a subjective experience, stirring in the objective spiritual streams at the present moment. It is of greater meaning that today some of you have formulated these subjective experiences in order for us to allow these to flow into our discussions during the next few days. You must not forget that in such a Movement, such as yours, it must be a question of working with real concrete spirits of the present time. What do people know about real spirit today? One of the most important facts for the support of inner spiritual activity in the present time will be the effect of people starting to see the indications given by Anthroposophy in America, which of course is unheard of. Now outer objects are being used to achieve insights.

Compare the world today with one of a hundred years ago. There are a multitude of differences, but one could say that one of the greatest differences is that today our atmosphere is crisscrossed either with telegraph or telephone wires. In Europe this entanglement of wires looks like a child's game compared to America. Here is a trace of possible insight regarding how that might affect people. Eventually one will sense that people are not immune to the activity buzzing through telephone wires in the air, making people into actual induction apparatuses. Consider an opposing stream in their nerves and then again one in the counter direction working in the bloodstream. All of this is what humanity carries in itself today, but it is hardly even noticed. These are pre-eminently Ahrimanic forces being absorbed by people from outer culture which they can't evade. One can think about things that are possible and impossible, and yet to the most powerful realities no thought is given. At some point the difference between Goethe and present day should be spoken about, regarding the fact that Goethe wasn't surrounded by telegraph wires. You see, the desolation of the human soul is in reality connected to all of this.

When you now look around at how the highest spiritual religious needs are satisfied, you must pose the question: Are there in these gratifications already some impulses inherent which take into account an element which renders these things harmless as part of the soul-spiritual experience? — That is not so! The satisfaction of religious needs go back to a time when all of this was not present, which I have illustrated for you. Today there is a gratification of religious needs which is only valid for a few people, which is not alive in the culture we have today. Anthroposophy wants to enter here to introduce newer impulses, impulses capable of making people independent from what they can't be independent of outwardly. What is external must be absorbed inwardly. Yet the polar opposite must be created — that means a strong awareness needs to be created for the importance of your Movement in order to create more and more impulses to come out of your Movement. The most important things must be thought through when you are to answer the question: What shall we do? — The correct application of the ritual and sermon already offers the necessary strong impulse because this religious Movement is built on the basis of Anthroposophy. Yet the awareness that humanity stands in the midst of these influences in the world must be present in every single one of us. Each one of you can contribute much towards fortifying awareness in this direction by raising it up and strengthen it.

We may not forget that gradually everything in humanity has become abstract and intellectual, and that intellectualism today stands completely in the afterglow. Today we may want to just understand things, but we must open our hearts for the realities of the spiritual world. Mere understanding, how this or that can be grasped, is all very good but it is not the reason for a movement to be supported. You see, some things need to be particularly perceived: those movements which are alert and equipped with strong will, sprouted from ancient humanity, have unbelievably deep roots in Central Europe and western folklore; the Roman Catholic Church is but one phase of this. Intellectualism having caused the desolation of the heart now results in crowds running in droves back to the existing church, namely the Catholic Church.

You are now only a small movement and few in numbers, but if you carry the awareness within you that you are working with Truth, then you will simply say to yourself: with spiritual movements it does not depend on how great they are in number but how strong their inner strengths are. This will be active when you have a strong awareness of what it is that is being carried. This is exactly what you must have: a strong consciousness for Truth and not allowing it to de-motivate you because in fact the truth is most detested. If you wish to spread some secular falsehood, then people will have no fear of it. Precisely when you want to spread the truth people sense your intention and there will be the strongest opposition you can find.

Today our intention is to examine two big oppositions. I don't want to refer to Jesuitism at every opportunity, also not in the usual sense; I mention it only as representative of the old spirituality penetrating present time in contrast to what modern culture has brought into the present. This stream promises the eradication of modern culture. You must not believe that the will forces in this Movement are insignificant. No doubt there is a striving to have humanity deprived of modern cultural elements, which is what this Movement carries. Modern cultural elements are considered as the devil which needs to be conquered by the old culture. Ahriman can't be eradicated but he can be refined, cleansed and made noble; he must be reckoned with alongside modern culture. Opponents know this as well and for this reason they clearly express their fear regarding your Movement because it contains truth. Errors soon come to nothing but by encountering the truth, the opposition grasp at anything in defence, big or small.

You can say that something has come out of Dornach which is connected to your Movement. However, I want to say without any ill meaning, that the destiny of the Goetheanum is also not without the link to your Movement originating from it. In the place where your actions come alive is where the burning spark is laid. Don't believe that your opposition works with limited resources. Above all we must be clear that our advancing impulse can't be located outwardly, nor can a deadening element be located externally. The one and only aspect of this Movement is its impulse of being in the inmost soul. Outer things can perhaps then take place tragically but there will be no obstacles for the impulse once it has been grasped and deepened and really expresses itself as it needs to do. It was a good impulse which has given an impetus to this religious Movement; it will express itself and bear fruit if it is continued forward with the same good sense. Now I will enter into some impulses coming from your midst, what you would like to discuss.

First Lecture

From the participants the following questions were brought:

1. How does our ritual relate to the cultic worship which will develop in the future? How should we work together in the right way with the Anthroposophic Movement? How can we do the right thing towards moral supportiveness of the overall Movement?

2. I ask for clarity regarding preceding historical events with particular reference to the Rhur district. (Rhurgebiet)

3. It doesn't help me to bring an objective balance to the ritual steps. They change as I practice it. The Act of Consecration of Man can be read in such a way as to physically link it to the nervous system but then it is not beneficial.

Rudolf Steiner: It is necessary to consider this last question or let someone else express it more precisely. For example, you speak a sentence, and it is not always clear if it has fulfilled the ritual of worship. That is a valid question. It needs to be looked at even closer. It would not be good to bring the nervous system into it. Naturally the act of worship must be on such a level that everything coming from it is not just on the level of the nervous system, which is already considered as far too important. ... (Gap in stenographer's notes.) In your subjective experience you must honour the objective experience flowing out of the ritual.

No uncertainty may limit speaking about the relationship of the ritual to anything else. The ritual which comes about, if you ask the spiritual worlds, is the ritual which lives within you. It is not in some or other outer exceptional form, but *it is the* ritual which is already finding its future but through life itself. The real inner involvement with the ritual is closely connected with the consciousness of the priest. The priest's consciousness can only develop when an inner honesty is outwardly present. Therefore, it would be good when the subjective soul aspect, experienced by individual personalities, as they work with the ritual, are openly spoken about on an occasion such as this. Only when you utter your subjective needs can we start talking in a fruitful way. ... (Gap in stenographer's notes.)

It boils down to the speech of the ritual being expressed as the speech of higher worlds. Human speech is from the outset an earthly speech because it finds expression in structured air. Of course, it is foolish to assume that departed souls can talk in a human way. Mediums in Germany let the spirits speak German, English in England and French in France as if one can be a German, English or a Frenchman after death. A spirit does no longer speak with a human language and can't pervade the air. What streams through speech as spirit depends on *how* it is spoken. At the very moment you have the feeling you are speaking with reverence then you can convey something spiritual through the spoken word. What does this mean: reverence? Reverence is something our philosophers have quite unlearned. They argue that the things they are discussing need to be grasped and touched. Whoever wants to speak about spiritual things must be aware that thought is like an etheric touch and that thoughts should be formed with reverence, just as also in the physical world, if it has to be touched with awe then it only is done on the surface. This inner feeling of reverence within speaking is of course the start. As a result, talking is then not only about content but physiognomic, it becomes conscious, and one can gradually become filled with the genius of speech. Through this, you start to discover talking itself as a living spiritual experience. This must be present in the ritual to the highest degree. Then you really stand within the process and therefore realize you are not speaking subjectively but you are a tool for the spiritual world.

On this rests the substantial understanding that it can be met with the ritual. Contributing most significantly to this is the *How* in the speech. This How however comes through the consciousness of being a tool for the spiritual world. Every small ritual action is a continuation of what flows out of the *Word*. In the ritual, these attribute to the words become gestures. Now the struggle surfaces in your awareness: You may think as you wish about something (this is irrelevant) but it comes down to you saying what the gods want you to say. Through this, one arrives at the point of awareness that the impulse of the Act of Consecration can be allowed to work through every little thing one does throughout the day.

What is this impulse? The impulse which comes out of the Act of Consecration lies essentially in the sacrifice/offering. In the sacrifice the earthly is offered to the spiritual world; we lay it down at the feet at the spiritual world. With communion we receive it again but now it comes out of the spiritual world. We have surrendered it out of the earthly. What happened in between? Transubstantiation: an exchange has happened with the spiritual world. This brings an awareness which allows us to stand within the spiritual world each time we experience the Act of Consecration. It is lifted higher by the Gospel reading preceding it. When the Gospel reading is a corresponding preparation for the interpenetration of the spiritual world between the offering and communion, then the right way to experience the Consecration of Man is found.

Of course, an addition is implicit to this: the Act of Consecration needs to be conducted at least every day. It is prescribed for Catholic priests to perform the Mass every day; through this they receive a powerful force. This must not be celebrated absolutely every day, but it is absolutely necessary that the Mass must be celebrated every day. Through this sensing you relate to the spiritual world. This is of the utmost importance.

Something else happens between one day and the next for priests: sleep happens between the two. What does this mean, sleep? Present day science has the peculiarity that the most important things in life make sense externally, but not inwardly. What is said about sleep is that it is an illusion. During sleep the soul-spiritual part of the human being, the 'I' and the astral body, are separated from the physical and etheric part. Between falling asleep and waking up the physical and ether bodies work on the level of the plant kingdom. What the human being has as remnant of the plant kingdom is found in his sleep, thus the human being descends as a physical being down to the plant level. This means processes are taking place which are of a lower kind than normal when a person is fully conscious. Something "cooks" up, warmth and cold are active in lower forces of nature which work in the same way where growth takes place. Only then do we have the right feeling when waking up — this must, of course, be perceived spiritually, otherwise it can be dangerous — when we say to ourselves: our I and astral bodies were in the divine world, our bodies we had handed down to the lower worlds; we then take the body back from the lower world which actually lies beneath the actual human world. This we must not forget; from an Ahrimanic level we take our bodies back, it is full of Ahrimanic build-up which we need to destroy during our waking hours. The first hour after waking should pass in such a way that we are capable of eradicating these things deposited overnight especially in for the form of salts in our bodies. When you don't manage this then the body becomes full of rheumatism, gout and so on, and on a soul level, full of lascivious thoughts. These things come from what has been experienced during sleep.

While the human being has sunk down (during sleep) to a level below that of humanity, the priest must now restore up to a higher level. This happens when the priest practices the ritual. One does not need, like in the Catholic church, to practice the Mass every day, but one should live within the Act of Consecration. That works as powerfully as the daily read mass. It then becomes powerful objectively. These are things we must observe in reality. It is essential that the human being sleeps every night. The Act of Consecration of Man is as important as sleep. If you occupy yourself every day with the Act if Consecration, you lift yourself out of the lower level of sleep-life. The evangelical attitude knows nothing about these things; it doesn't want to lift priests out but want them to remain on the level of nightly sleep-life. This lifting out of people from their nightly life of sleep, this conscious opposition to the sinking down of people into their lower human consciousness, this is what actually constitutes the vocation of priests.

What is the level on which human beings exist? The human level lies between the plant and animal regions, also between air and water. The human being is firstly mineral, plant-like, animal-like; not yet actually human. The human being will only be formed in future. When we meditate through the Mass, we don't enter the animal-like aspect but enter into the divine which otherwise can only work unconsciously in us. If we carry around with us only what is daily consciousness — yes, you see, we would not look like we look now, we would only have a body developed up to the diaphragm, men would have heads like bulls and women would have heads of lions. What we have in our day consciousness doesn't enable us to have a human physical head — that is given to us by the divine. For this reason, we see the embryo head as developed to a high degree. During normal waking hours we can't entirely embrace our total human form, but we learn to take this human form which is godly, to really experience the earth. You only come to have the right to feel yourself positioned in the human physiognomy when you lift yourself out of the animalistic, during the Mass. Then you free yourself from the animal and lion nature and as a result, have a human-godly physiognomy.

This is where the Catholic Church is insistent — for the divine to speak through the human. When you start to become the practical performer of the ritual then you need to grasp these things infinitely more earnestly than in the normal sense; to the extreme it is necessary to look at it and say to yourselves: we don't carry a human head when we interact with ordinary people, because the divine works in the human head.

For this reason, it is why the "Act of Consecration" is not a poor expression but a good one, a very good one. How your head is positioned in the world is not due to your doing, but God created it thus. Ordination means taking what is firm and making it fluid, what the individual has is baptised into the spiritual. As a result, you can say: I earn the right to live in the divine through the Act of Consecration and meditation and thus allow the members of the congregation to only take part in the Act of Consecration and meditation. This doesn't contradict the social and also not the evangelical consciousness but in fact it is the right attitude to reality. Only thereby it is contradicted that you turn yourself away from the things in the ordinary world; yet by consciously juxtaposing yourself to it, you conquer it. There is always more to strive for, more to struggle through and understand because priest consciousness is not a given from one day to the next, you must first allow these things to permeate you.

A speech exercise is asked for.

Rudolf Steiner: The Catholic Church considers language seriously and insists on speech exercises. The Jesuit must recite and learn to scan, he must learn how to shape an opening sentence and a concluding sentence, how to prepare the initial sentence in order to be convincing with the second one and by ending without impoverishing it by lack of eloquence. Speech becomes something objective. Speech for most people is only an expression of a purely physical organ — the larynx and the mucous membranes. The spoken word which is to be practiced in the ritual must make itself free from the individual, it must have its foundation as a power to vibrate the air without allowing the mucus to mix into it. Today this is not something that can be done effortlessly; it needs practice. The Berlin University once had a professor of eloquence, called Ernst Curtius, but so little was known in that time that he never fulfilled this lectureship but instead recited Greek art history.

The Essence of the Active Word

Second Lecture

Stuttgart, 12 July 1923

My dear friends!

Perhaps deepening some of the questions of yesterday can be our starting point today. Dr Rittelmeyer has already called our attention to some difficulties which exist in understanding the relationship of this Christian-religious Movement to Anthroposophy. These difficulties are such that you actually can't just through, one could call it a definition, try and deal with it, but that it should actually be dealt with through practical application, and then also through a certain study of soul relationships in present-day humanity. The soul relationships in present-day humanity have only really just emerged in the course of the last three to four centuries and far too little consideration has been given to exploring just how difficult these soul relationships really are. Thus you must already be clear about how, out of all the energy and best of will impulses a religious movement can be formed, which can also work powerfully and nonetheless in opposition to other movements of our time where the hearts of people have gradually become lost, if at the same time the needs of humanity were not satisfied by the older, or relatively not so very old, religious streams having become unavailable.

We may not give in to the illusion that in reality it would be possible to lead a religious movement separated from the rest of cultural life, namely, to be apart from what is called scientific culture. You must be aware that an atheistic science armed with the highest authority exists today. Now you would probably say, sure, this atheistic science exists as a science, but alongside that some or other contemporary science and those involved there insist they are filled not with a contemporary but an inner piousness; so that there are possibly people who can live quite within this present day atheistic scientific community who say: 'This is another field but when I'm not active in this field then I find myself in a religious life.'

You see, this separation between the scientific and the religious elements which has been going on for centuries, this inner separation can still not cope with such a strong and pure Movement as yours — because a religious movement must, just like a scientific movement, above all support the truth. It can now seem even trivial when, after having spoken so much about the content of a religious movement, we again return to the elementary idea: the Movement must be truthful. We may not undervalue how strong the present-day untruthfulness, the inner unconscious falsehood of civilisation has become. What the first initiators of this Religious Movement felt at the time, when they made the suggestion for founding this Movement, was in reality precisely towards dealing with that inner, unconscious untruthfulness of our present day.

You see, out of the cultural historical discomfort the view has gradually been developed that one must leave science to science; the theologians need not bother with it. The theologians had to create their own principles of truth from which they developed ethical and religious content separated from anything scientific and gradually introduced eternity and religiosity while not bothering with what drove science. It is exactly this detachment of the religious life placing itself opposite cultural life which resulted in deep inner untruth. Those who practice science as it is carried out today can only be atheists if he or she is honest because the manner and way thoughts regarding the world, as it is carried out in physics and chemistry, give no possibility to rise up to any kind of ethic ideal. There exists only one truth for the science of today, namely: "The totality of the world is determined by causes. The world of causality is however neutral towards ethic and religious ideals, completely neutral. Right here we must search for the truth and conclude there is no other way than to remain with the verdict of astronomers: I have searched through the entire universe and haven't found God anywhere; I therefore don't need this hypothesis." Something else is not possible for science, if one is really honest.

On the basis of such a scientific viewpoint depends how a question such as: "Should we abandon everything moral and ethical?" is answered in the following way: "If we do this then humanity will fall into chaos and therefore it is necessary to tame humanity from the outside with state laws or equivalents." We then have tamed people where the principle of being tamed becomes nothing other than a higher form of submission just like one applies to animals. Religion, for people who thought like this, only had one entitlement and that was to use it as a means to activate people into mutual opposition. Religion was just a means to an end; only this was allowed by those with a scientific way of thinking regarding the present. A large part of those who undermined humanity like this is as a result of not having an honest disgust for a way of thinking which only takes the half, that is, the scientific method of thought and incidentally invents the theory of how humanity was tamed. When one speaks about religious and ethical impulses with only this attitude then one must be completely clear that all one can speak about are the taming rules. One always steers towards deeper untruthfulness if one doesn't confess these things. On the other hand, atheistic science can't be stopped. Just think how forcefully today intentions arise to establish human institutions solely and extensively based on mere materialistically thought-out inherited principles, for example laws set up for marriage where nothing about inner heartfelt relationships are the decisive factor, but rather, for example, that a doctor decides. These things are argued away but in reality, these things do not have an end. For those who want to work from the basis of religious renewal it is necessary to be clear to unite the focus of knowledge simultaneously with the spirit into nature's wisdom, making the spirit prevalent within the wisdom of nature so that right into physics spirituality is alive. This need really be striven for by the fact that the religious movement is based on Anthroposophy. Still, this basis of Anthroposophy needs to be a totally inward, truthful aspect. For this reason, it is necessary that the relationship between the Religious Renewal and Anthroposophy is also represented in the correct way.

Isn't it true that Anthroposophy wants and can't be anything other than a quest for knowledge? You must, also as far as your relationship involves its followers, be fully aware that you are working with a path of knowledge. The religious renewal is even a religious movement with a corresponding religious ritual. When both movements work out of their own impulses then only mutual fructification can result. Basically, this can never cause trouble. One must, when one is clear about it, know that on the whole, trouble can't appear when the conditions of the time are considered. The Anthroposophical Movement can be seen to have a difficult position because many people thirst for a spiritualised world view and spiritualised knowledge but want to come to their knowledge with more comfort and ease than what Anthroposophy offers. People don't want such intensive inner work which is necessary in Anthroposophy and as a result really absurd points of view and thoughts pop up. It is like this — you only need to remind yourselves about yesterday's lecture — for those who really want to be involved with Anthroposophy, a basic rethink is necessary which creates a radical difference between Anthroposophists and those who have no inkling of the existence of such rethinking and transformative sensitivity.

Second Lecture

What actually makes a community? A communal thinking and feeling! One can hardly imagine that people who truthfully work with the Anthroposophical impulse would not get such a feeling of community, as it had never before been in the world. Such a fundamental change in thinking has never existed before, even in the Mysteries: then everything was quite similar to popular thought. There is a strong bond where everyone calls and shouts for community which often becomes evident among the youth, surfacing basically as an absurd tendency. However, don't forget we are not in a studio where we can make people out of plasticine, but that people exist out there in all their absurdities, which one need to refer back to, from which there is no escape if one wants to do real work. It comes down to taking these things profoundly and in all seriousness. One tends not to think about all the various fields. Perhaps you will understand me better if I give you a popular example.

In the Waldorf School we now have 12 Classes and students of up to the age of 18 or 19. They all want to be teachers. Now, the first and foremost requirement in teaching and education lies in the non-discussion of the teaching methods to the child, boy or girl; these methods need to remain a mystery. The way things are accomplished these days centre around the child in the Waldorf School; revealing the pedagogical foundation and so on to them as they are growing up until they sometimes know what Waldorf pedagogy is better than the teacher. Yes, when things are like this there can be no progress.

On the other hand, it is not acceptable today to dissect things in an outer manner. Recently in a delegation meeting we spoke about the method of how money could be acquired for the reconstruction (of the Goetheanum). A hateful article appeared as a result in a Geneva newspaper in a wild attack, how the poor Swiss people were having a million Franks pulled out of their pockets. Open secrets also don't work. It must come down to the ability to inwardly depend on people, so that when basic rules of secrecy are not given, that a form of tact develops among the authoritative personalities, speaking about something in a specific way and not, for instance, reveal the ground rules of Waldorf pedagogy to a fifteen-year-old as one would to a thirty-year-old person. This must gradually come out of it. In fact, all kinds of absurd added impulses come to the fore, when things are not considered in depth or with enough strength.

This is how the impulse for community building appears in the Anthroposophical Movement. The Anthroposophical Movement is a movement for knowledge. It is founded on the communality of will, feeling and thought. Thus, one can actually consider that the Religious Movement would simply rise out of the foundation of the Anthroposophical Movement, taken up in the way which was once given to religious movements which had come out of archetypal impulses and then developed further.

Before any religious movement existed among the Anthroposophists, a substitute was looked for in all kinds of esoteric circles which were however based solely on knowledge and the aspect considered as ritualistic also was just there to serve knowledge. As a result, nothing from these circles could be brought across into a movement for the renewal of religion.

Had things going on at that time, considered then as ritualistic, had these things not been permeated with the pulse of knowledge, they would have been conceived outwardly which is not where they had their origin.

In contrast it is namely so in religious movements, that the ritual itself contains immediate content in each act of worship so that those who for instance refuse to strive for knowledge within the ritual, still through their participation in the ritual shares in the ritual's life, because the ritual, in the way it should work in this Religious Movement, is the speech of the spiritual world,

Second Lecture

brought down into earthly form, making participation in the ritual something quite positive.

Let us contemplate the central focus of the ritual from this viewpoint. When we look at the Act of Consecration, we notice the preparatory part being the Gospel reading. Now here is another difficulty because it is really necessary to get a better understanding of the Gospels than what currently exists. It is really a matter of understanding that the Words of the Gospels are to be taken up quite differently to any other words, which have flowed from civilisation's development through humanity. The Word of the Gospel, when it is taken as the truth, contains within itself something which can be described when one says: The person who reads the Words of the Gospel out loud, speaks as the conduit for something which comes down from the spiritual into the physical world in order for the prepared part of the Gospel text to somehow enable the entire congregation to establish a link to the spiritual world.

Following this, the actual offering takes place, in three parts: Revelation, Transubstantiation and Communion. A real conception of this trinity is not possible if one is not clear about the very moment when transubstantiation is fulfilled, even for those who actually take part, when natural law and ethical law flow together as one, so that quite a different world order is opened up every time for the congregation, each moment when a person is lifted up to the divine, and the spiritual sinks down into the congregation. When one takes this as reality then one must say, something is happening which is completely independent to what one can *recognise* as happening in it. Mere feeling is sufficient for what precedes it. For knowledge, mere feeling is insufficient. For the preparatory steps to transformation, it suffices to have feeling, therefore actually it is a task, an activity involving the congregation, when the priest celebrates the Act of Consecration for the congregation. This is something which must definitely be accepted and as a result you should never disturb this harmony by asking the question: 'Could any ritual which is received today out of the spiritual world' — and all our rituals are received from the spiritual world are to some extent ordained by God — 'can it be changed or stopped?' — You see, by somehow evaluating these rituals and come to saying: 'Yes, it should develop into another state where people can have an invisible ritual' — these questions are unreasonable.

The relationship must be thought of in this way: people are always going to look for a ceremony followed by a sermon; in the sermon the only enrichment flowing into it can come from Anthroposophy, out of spiritual science. It will happen in future that those who are knowledgeable in the <u>topmost degree</u> in spiritual matters, will never reject keeping community with those who attend the ritual. He or she has also no other way of relating to the ritual than, I could call it, a naive person. Therefore, the question can't possibly be raised: 'Do we carry the ritual for the present time and in future substitute it by another?' — Through our founding of the ritual it is established and will continue; it is subject to other rules than those that human beings validate when it is asked: 'Will there one day be an invisible ritual?' The Ritual is subjected to the immense cosmic world impulses which include everything in its evolution which comes about in the world. However, the changes of the future will be quite different to changes that have happened in the past.

Take the Mass of the today's Roman Catholic Church. What is present there is the synthetic confluence of all the corresponding rituals of ancient times, deepened in a Christian sense. This is the wonderful element within the Catholic Church which has flowed together out of all the ancient mysteries. However, at specific times in the development of Christianity there came about — these times actually already began in the third and fourth century — times during which there was no understanding any more for

Second Lecture

what was woven into the sacrifice of the Mass and so it became an empty formula, propagating itself through tradition, one could say, out of respect. Then, seemingly soon, people came with the courage of non-understanding and started to improve all kinds of things. Today, as a result, we have in the Catholic Mass sacrifice, something which gradually, simply through the dying out of language, has become fundamentally incomprehensible. It is celebrated in the old language, without it possibly bringing about understanding. One can regard this sacrifice of the Catholic Mass as a corpse, which is something unthinkably huge and powerful, yet still as a corpse possessing unbelievable power. In totality the peculiar aspect of the Catholic Church is how the priesthood is exceptionally educated philosophically but theologically extraordinarily uneducated. The Catholic theology has no liveliness, so that actually right up to the greatest climaxes Catholic theology is something extraordinarily uneducated. Since the Middle Ages it hasn't undergone any further development. On the grounds of religious needs of humanity, the teaching or sermon all fail to be satisfying, yet by contrast this is not the case with the cult because the cult has an extraordinary power of building the community. This is what is given in which you can engender a feeling of eternity through this new ritual, so that no disharmony needs to bear down on your souls. Some Anthroposophists claim that parts of the prescribed ritual can be left out. This question would actually not come about if one has the right attitude. I really don't know out of what grounds these ideas could have come. Because take the case of the funeral today; surely a religious community will ask for a ritual? So you are called to the Consecration of Man for the whole of humanity and not only with the attitude that it is something temporary, it will be replaced by something else. This is something eternal as far as something can be called eternal on earth. This conflict which appears to be developing among many of you, that

Anthroposophy sees the ritual to some extent as something less meaningful or that something else in the future must represent the present Movement, this conflict can only be based on a feeling of a misunderstanding. As soon as you are clear that naturally Anthroposophy lies more on the side of knowledge and that it must give itself over to that, as far as the ritual is considered, then on the other side, people who attend the ritual and also seek the knowledge aspect, because of the strength of the intellect, and approach the ritual from the basis of Anthroposophy — as soon as you are clear about this then you can say to yourself in some way this is only a kind of division of labour. If taken from this basis, conflict should not arise at all.

Now I would like to ask you, following on from these comments, to express whatever you want because I know that much still lies in the depths of your souls.

A question is posed (*which is not written down by the stenographer*) regarding the lecture given on the 31st of December 1922 in Dornach.

A Saying:

The world's working approaches
As a material reflection to me
In the Heavenly Beings of the stars
I see, through Willing, their loving motion.
Penetrating me with life's water
Forming me through matter's power
The heavenly deeds of the stars
Within feeling I see their wise revolving.

Es nahet mir im Erdenwirken
In Stoffes Abbild mir gegeben
Der Sterne Himmelswesen
Ich seh' im Wollen sie sich liebend wandeln.

Second Lecture

Es dringen in mich im Wasserleben
In Stoffes Kraftgewalt mich bildend
Der Sterne Himmelstaten
Ich seh' im Fühlen sie sich weise wandeln.

Rudolf Steiner: What I spoke about then is a kind of cosmic communion. When this is performed meditatively, then under the circumstances as things are today, they could offer people a certain satisfaction. In this way a kind of communion can be received. However, that doesn't exclude those who receive communion through their knowledge in this way, when they in their entire soul constitution strive for it today, to also receive communion in another way. The differences should not be stressed because the two things are not contradictory. Do you experience a stronger contradiction here than what you have against the old, still truly understood, Catholic Church? There they have the priest communion and naturally also the lay communion — I don't want to say that all Anthroposophists should be priests. You have those who can give and receive communion and you have those who can receive communion but not give it. When you grasp the difference, you have to say to yourself: 'Those who give communion can't possibly, without it adding some inner experience, take the communion anyhow like the layman. He must experience something more in it.' Therefore, the priest, when working with the communion, must also experience something more, an inner communion, and this he does have. Now, it comes down to strictly adhering to the difference between the priesthood and the laity. Only these two classes exist. Today one walks away from the developments in these olden times, this past time is no longer here.

Today much which was only available to the Priests in olden times is now to some extent also made available to the laity. Our entire modern theology, all its literature is now available. The same can be said to be valid in our case. You can study theology as a layman. If you choose a way of knowledge like Anthroposophy it is self-evident that the thoughts of participants become familiar with such things as would first and foremost been available for the celebrating Priests in past times. Today it is different. We can't put up boundaries. If we would have clung to old principles it would be as if a religious movement existed and within that movement would have been the priesthood who then would have Anthroposophy to themselves, who would have to do everything on the level of profane technicality, as demanded by the times ... (*gap in stenographer's notes*). If you take that into account, you will understand that this communion which the priest celebrates has developed from something which belongs to the Anthroposophical Movement. However, there is no ground for saying: 'On the one hand we have the priestly, on the other we have cosmic communion.' Both come from the same foundation, only differentiating in form. They can both stand independently beside one another. So, when you enter with profound feeling into these things you will have no difficulties.

A Participant: In the report about the meeting of delegates in February 1923, it is said that the ritualistic element is something which comes from prenatal life. In the course which we attended in Dornach, it is illustrated how our ritual raises up the dead in their life after death.

Rudolf Steiner: This is something which is applicable to all things created out of the spiritual world; the concepts need to be grasped very precisely. To grasp concepts scholarly dialectic needs to be entered into. However, we haven't come that far yet, neither in the area of Anthroposophy, nor in the Religious Movement. You see, the way people work in the ritual, to really engage, so that the human soul is involved, is in order for this to lead to the Portal of Death and encounter Christ — this is the one side of the cult. The

Second Lecture

other side through which that takes place for the human being is like a cosmic memory of what had been experienced prenatally. Let's take an example in ordinary life to make this clear. What meeting makes a great impression on a person today? To have had an encounter, already during his youth, with a venerated person. Now something else is added to this. It is something different, when I depict it, which germinates in the mood of soul towards the future; as a result of this he might approach relationships in life in quite a different manner to the kind of person he had been in his youth. When one partakes in the ritual, one's next, future life is touched. This happens because its origin lies in prenatal life. This works very strongly on the human being.

A Participant: Does one accomplish more by meditating on the Mass or when one celebrates the Mass? One can then come as far as saying we don't need to read the Mass anymore.

Rudolf Steiner: Logically that is not quite untrue, but in fact it is not so. When the Mass is read and is then experienced meditatively and thus has an effect on you, then this effect, while depending on a more intense inner activity, actually becomes stronger. However, you are not always able to call upon this inner activity. When you haven't read the Mass for some days then its power becomes paralysed. It is true, if one can, then it is good, but when it has had no preparatory stages then these forces are paralysed. It is not true that the inner meditated Mass is as strong as the read Mass, and it must not somehow become an ideal for the Priest, to not read the Mass. Then he could well say: 'I refrain from working with my congregants, I, alone, want to make progress.' It is possible to imagine this ideal (not reading the Mass but meditating) but the power which the priest will need, when he wants to read the Mass, this he must not allow to weaken as a result, by him wanting to present such an ideal.

A participant: How does one bring people to the Consecration of

Man? Are we to only take people who emotionally come from underdeveloped religious sentiments, to whom the way of knowledge is closed? How should we approach participants if we don't follow the route of thinking?

Rudolf Steiner: You don't just have the ritual, but also in the broadest sense the sermon, lectures, or preaching in the terminological sense. Nothing can be seen as a problem. Today's younger intellectuals who work out of nothing don't want an isolated intellectual aspect but strive strongly towards ritual.

What can enter here, which must from external sources form a synthesis between the Religious Movement and Anthroposophy, I now want to characterise. On the one hand today's intellect is not enlivened without the ritual. The ritual firstly calls upon the intellect. Today people stop believing they can think if they don't have the ritual. Stopping thinking is a danger of the time. On the other hand, I don't see where the limitation must lie when presenting a sermon and ritual. A limitation can only exist where you create it artificially. They don't want to learn about Anthroposophy, they say. That they can't handle because they must! Of course, one should not throw Anthroposophy at them because then the problem arises with them saying: 'We don't want to learn about Anthroposophy.'

A participant: So, we won't talk about the ether body, for example?

Rudolf Steiner: That depends on the knowledge of the congregation. I can easily imagine a congregation who relate honestly to the ritual and still can have a need for knowledge. I don't see why you shouldn't speak about the ether body.

A participant: There are actually people with a desire for knowledge and who find their way to Anthroposophy through the ritual. Can we find a possibility to satisfy people who don't want Anthroposophy?

Second Lecture

Rudolf Steiner: The question is actually: how will you characterise someone who should be led by you, who will actually be led by you in order for that person to be seen quite separated from Anthroposophy? How must that person be? It is like this: When one really grasps what a person is about, when one really enters into true humanity, then people want Anthroposophy, just as at all times the underlying soul is being sought for. To not want Anthroposophy is only the case with inhibited people. For forty years you could still find elementally healthy people in the countryside, they uttered the highest wisdom. (*The following sentence was only partially captured*.) Under their pillows they use to hide something — take Jacob Böhme for instance — this is no longer found today. People who have become inhibited in large cities don't come anywhere near such things. As a result, I can imagine that another way can be used, other than anthroposophic. Your approach need not be from what is printed in books but what you have experienced through books. For example, the concept of the etheric body is easy to bring across to naive individuals. In some regions people called the little substance left in the eyes upon waking, "night's sleep"; the etheric is in there because it comes from the etheric body's activity. Starting points are everywhere. You satisfy people more when you become free of words and come from experience itself.

A participant: Is it possible to find the difference between cosmic communion and the ritual in order to formulate it as sacramental?

Rudolf Steiner: That is something which is difficult to say, because experience of real cosmic communication is already sacramental. All of anthroposophic thought is something sacramental, as I have expressed it already in my *Goethean Science*. Knowledge, when it is true knowledge, strives towards sacrament. It depends more upon us trying to bring things together than to find differences, because in reality you bring yourself together with it.

THE ESSENCE OF THE ACTIVE WORD

A question is posed with reference to specific words in a sentence from one of Rudolf Steiner's Dornach lectures of 1922 (indicated by a few connecting words by the stenographer).

Rudolf Steiner: 'Anthroposophy needs no religious renewal' — so you have correctly formulated the sentence. What will it mean for Anthroposophy, whose foundation is in itself, to need religious renewal? The reverse: 'Religious renewal needs Anthroposophy!' What was said there in the lecture, that Anthroposophy needs ritual, was actually directed at Anthroposophists, not at the Movement for Religious Renewal. Such things need to be said because many people believe they need to orientate themselves out of principle, whether they should choose to take part in the Religious Movement. There were members of the Anthroposophic Movement who were much older than Dr Rittelmeyer; when they asked if they should take part in the ritual, one must say to them: 'In the end you should know this yourself, *you* must be able to consult Dr Rittelmeyer.' — One may not say that the only way to come to anthroposophy is through the Religious Movement; that would be very wrong. My lecture at that time was directed at Anthroposophists. It is therefore self-evident that the Anthroposophists, as they have become lately, could be consultants for the ritual. The opposite is deadly for Anthroposophy: when you say one couldn't come to an anthroposophic understanding (of Christ) if you do not come via the ritual. It is necessary to stress that the lecture was directed at Anthroposophists. The misunderstanding came about by *both* sides making mistakes of omission in their handling. There are many in the Religious Movement who doesn't know what they should be doing.

Marie Steiner: Some Anthroposophists created the saying: "Dr Steiner wants the Religious Movement to replace the Anthroposophical movement"; that was Dr Steiner's assessment. Similarly at the start of the Threefold Movement it was also

Second Lecture

suggested it should replace the Anthroposophical Movement. There have already been signs of people believing that Anthroposophy should be disassembled. Lecture cycles at the publishers were cancelled, and such like.

Rudolf Steiner: These things appear in outer practice and do not lead to inner difficulties.

A Participant pointed out that Rudolf Steiner had said during the lecture on 30 December 1922 that there were many people who are orientated towards knowledge but other people with dull religious inclination (*text here only copied in key words by the stenographer*).

Rudolf Steiner: Yes, that can't be denied, there are people with a thorough orientation towards knowledge and others with just a dull religious inclination. If I said that Anthroposophy can't do anything with people who have dull religious instincts, but only through something like the Religious Movement, then it is true. However, it does not mean that the Religious Movement is applicable to only these kinds of people, but it means these people can't do anything with Anthroposophy. These people can only be reached through the ritual, not through Anthroposophy. People with a dull religious inclination are to be involved through the ritual and possibly will become very thoughtful people in their next lives.

A participant: People say: 'The Anthroposophists have a university, you have a school for children.' This is the kind of thing we have to deal with.

Rudolf Steiner: Recently I saw a big poster which came out of Austria with sheer nonsense on it, claiming how concerned individuals reach the spiritual world, but on the other side it said: 'With my spiritual system I include all things which are only approached one-sidedly by Anthroposophy and Theosophy etc.'

With such things inner difficulties can't be judged. Such people one may not take as tragic. You can't be upset by this.

A participant: To prevent such things being proclaimed, the leader of the branch needs to take action.

Rudolf Steiner: These are outer things. The leader of branch is not involved with what members do outside the branch.

A participant: It is said directly that the two paths are contradictory. This frightens people and they stay away.

Rudolf Steiner: This is not inner difficulty, it is outer action of practical life. That these things happen cannot be stopped. One can't characterise something in a trivial way which is connected to the most serious profundity; for this is needed clear formulation, with serious words which can possibly appear as falsely expressed. What one or another branch leader has to say is quite insignificant. Otherwise, we have to regard it as a task to only have branch leaders who are infallible. Your spiritual tools are there to educate people.

Emil Bock: In a certain sense there was no confusion in the beginning. We were looking for our field of work as somewhere different from the Anthroposophic field. We probably took the declarations of the opposition as our connecting point which made us too separate from the Anthroposophic work. Some of us also had no more time for it. As a result of these difficulties arising among the Anthroposophists we realised we could not speak from the side of Anthroposophists. As a result of the course of events we had separated ourselves somewhat out of the anthroposophical line. Now we ask you, please help us, to find the true way in the anthroposophic work again, because we have a strong desire not to fall away from the Anthroposophic work and see how as a result we have attracted the possibility to really contribute to the clarification of us not being seen as

Second Lecture

Anthroposophists but as standing for Religious Renewal. We do not want to be poor representatives of Anthroposophy.

Rudolf Steiner: The danger was actually there from the beginning. It all depends on the correct critical attitude being maintained. It is possible through many things that judgement is rectified. For several months already, Dr Rittelmeyer is very actively involved in the Management (Forstand) of the Anthroposophic Society. What he says is highly recommended. It is already so that the strength of each one of you becomes strongly recommended. I will never again, at an occasion where social relationships are to be healed by the ritual, participate without a representative of the Religious Movement working with me. At burials I will no longer speak alone, without a priest. The ritual needs to be celebrated by the priest. In this way correct judgement must be built up. In discussions misunderstandings arrive, but the facts speak for themselves.

It is important that the Religious Movement does not deny Anthroposophy. You are mistaken if you believe you can make progress without it. It is far better to be clear and stand firm on the foundation of Anthroposophy. Everything must be openly brought to light. You may not allow people to come to the opinion that it has nothing to do with Anthroposophy. The Waldorf School is completely related to Anthroposophy. Some lecturer has said that the Waldorf School is quite nice if only their basic views could be dropped.

It is this which I want to stress: If Anthroposophy is the foundation of the Waldorf School, then we don't create an anthroposophic sect education, but by going through Anthroposophy we strive towards a general education of mankind.

We have the task not to clarify misunderstandings but simply to speak the truth.

THE ESSENCE OF THE ACTIVE WORD

Third Lecture

Stuttgart, 13 July 1923

My dear friends!

For the kind of striving you are involved in, it is of primary importance to cultivate a true impulse for feeling yourselves within the spiritual world as well as striving towards the achievement of such an impulse, but taken from the viewpoint of your Movement, of which I intend speaking to you today. You see it really involves establishing a connection with a definite point to enable you to link to a spiritual impulse, if you want to be a sure, broad minded, active person, which you all want to be. It involves enlivening the appropriate impulses for this particular activity. From my observations in the spiritual world as such, it appears that the following will be helpful to you.

A connection can be established with the manifestation of the spirit of speech, the wielding of the speech genius. We must firstly be very clear, my dear friends, how far we are removed as a rule from the real spiritual, inner self-activation of grasping speech within ourselves. We basically are involved with speech but without its divine quality. We take up speech in such a manner that by the very act of applying it to ordinary life, we actually profane it. We allow ourselves as contemporary people to use speech by not venerating it in any way at all. We basically speak in sinfulness, and this can awaken the awareness that our speaking sinfully enables us to acquire an attitude, I may say, to develop a relationship with speech towards obtaining a spiritual impulse. Examples to confirm this arise of course from all areas.

The Essence of the Active Word

How many people today have obtained some guidance which empathises with any of the sounds in speech? This naturally means a large number of sounds are spoken conventionally and inhumanely, without comprehension, uttered as if without human input. Who feels at the moment the word "harden" is spoken, that in expressing the word the speaker's mood is permeated by something which hardens it like a mineral and simultaneously cools down his mood? Who feels, when the word "Word" is spoken that it is linked to life from ancient times, a past spiritual weaving which has been killed in the present time, the past crystallized in the present, and so on? We have absolutely no experience of the most important words anymore. I would like to know how many people today have the experience with the word "thinking," how many people have an experience with the word "feeling," the word "willing." This I'm only saying to you with reference to what I really want to entrust you with today.

You may of course name yourself in the most varied expressions of language. You can call yourself "I" as one does usually, or you can start to theorise about it and say to yourself you can be called a "human-being" (Mensch)(1). Then you substitute the speech genius and determine your own being out of the being of the language. However today a person has the feeling when he does something like that, he is applying a word which he designates to himself. When a person of today says to himself he can be called a "human-being," he thinks that under all circumstances he has in a comprehensive way with a word, he believes, described an idea.

Now, when the starting point is feeling, it is good: in the true sense of the word language is so little understood, making the description which a person as a human-being applies to himself actually something whose understanding must first be wrestled with, whose understanding must first be arrived at. Feeling should actually always be a starting point so that when I believe I

Third Lecture

can describe myself in some or other words, even in my mother tongue, they designate an infinite pride in me. When we permeate ourselves with the feeling that we believe we can manage a language, even our mother tongue, so far removed from the spirit that we can legitimately name ourselves with the word "human-being," if we consider this belief as terribly proud then we start to draw courage for the preparatory feeling towards a specific spiritual impulse such as I am indicating today. We should much more often be able to say: 'I am placed on the earth as a human-being through some or other divine circumstances unknown to me and this leads me to call myself a "human-being," but the basis for this description lies high above my horizon. It is the will of God who prevails here, who has led me out of the unconscious deep substrate, to describe me as "human-being." I have as a human-being, as this human individuality standing on earth, actually not the right to characterize myself.' Then the next step must be to say to oneself: Before I can become capable at all of understanding the entire preliminary stages in existence which leads to me saying "I" to myself, I must undergo three developmental steps — right up to the judgement which I may express as the following: I have no right to call myself "human-being," I need to first go through three steps of development, I must push through three tests. When I have passed these three tests to satisfy my own judgement, will I have earned the right to say to myself: 'You are a human-being.'

This we should actually feel toward every spoken word: an extraordinary noble humility towards the point of origin for the development of spiritual impulses. We need to say to ourselves: Just like we as human beings stand on earth today in our 5th Post-Atlantean period, we may, if we are honest people, start by falling quiet, name nothing and then start to conquer the three steps which will give us the right to rename things out of ourselves. Through this can we first get a feeling for how extraordinary a meaningful cosmic experience it had been, as indicated in scripture, that in the presence of God Adam was permitted to name animals and things, which only God's proximity could enable. We come through such experiences which need indeed to be concrete personal experiences, to the necessary depths of the scripture, so that it, through its inner power which we can give it, reach the necessary nuances and coloration and out of every word in each verse let it ring out, to which we can't merely say: 'We don't have the right to name things' — but we could say: 'Through God the right has been given to us, to name things out of ourselves.'

These things must firstly be experienced through the depths of our soul in a priestly way to really encounter the world. Outer gestures do not make a priest, because the priest expresses what comes out of the deepest depths within. When we designate the words "human-being" as such to ourselves, we should only be able to do so when we have gone through these three stages:

> The being to whom I want to ascribe the word "human-being" has depths which I must first need to fathom;

> The being to whom I want to ascribe the word "human-being" has heights to which I need to rise first;

> The being to whom I want to ascribe the word "human-being" has widths which I first have to look at and grasp.

These three sentences contain something meaningful: *being* a human-being. By deepening these sentences through meditation, they can take you a long way.

In truth it is so: by the human-being placing himself in earthly existence he places himself outside spiritual heights. Solely through the fact that our earth existence is a cooperative task towards human development, cosmically validated, do we contribute a part of our totality as earthlings. Earth shapes us

Third Lecture

while we walk on it between birth and death, as earthlings, and everything which is shaped out of the earth come out of the depths which cooperates in everything, even in the most minute parts of the smallest organs in us. Just imagine the earth as a being in space has endless secrets within it which work creatively. How your eyes, your ears are formed, how every singular, how every smallest member of your body is formed and fashioned, for all this the creative forces lie within the earth. If we succeed in gradually grasping what the earth's expression of its inner being is in its countenance, with thinking, feeling and willing as an unveiling of her inner secrets, so we meditatively, gradually come to search for an answer to the question: How do I fathom the depths of the being of man?

When we succeed in placing ourselves into our bodies as the multitudinous ways of crystallised earth, which dissolves the crystallisation again, atomised to a powder, when we succeed in observing this development, pulverising and re-crystalling which in the course of time was characterised for the sensitive human-being, for example with Brahma, Vishnu, Shiva; if we succeed in experiencing this entire process which will be for us a kind of bed of the Godhead, by us being embedded in it, so that the bedding within this Brahma-Vishnu-Shiva process becomes something like a cosmic sleep for us during our earth existence, if we experience this crystallisation and dissolving as something which weaves through us with a cosmic urge for sleep, so that we could say: the human-being is so profound, so deeply fashioned in earthly existence that the depths of consciousness doesn't endure but with the entire created earth as a physical body it expires into a cosmic sleep — then we gradually approach the feeling of what it means: what it is for the human-being to be connected to the depths of the earth. If we can finally say to ourselves: the earth forms us out of its depths, permeates us out of its depths with earthly sleep, while out of the depths of earthly sleep the archetypal divine works fully consciously, then we experience something of these earthly depths within the human-being. If we could say something like the harder the earth appears to us, diamond hard, the harder in its parts, just so more true, so powerfully speaks from this diamond hard heart the condition of sleep of the spiritual world, the light filled spirituality which works in the earth as awakened, active divinity.

Thus, we need to go through our meditation in an ever more deepening feeling way and transfer the earthly foundation and say:

'Oh man, before you can name yourself, before you can establish your depths, you need to ever more deepen yourself into the foundations of the earth.' When we observe plants sprouting out of the earth, we may acquire a loftier feeling of piety, a feeling of reverence, that in every plant morsel we can behold something of ourselves, something like a revelation of what is happening below in the earth. We must really clearly understand the exchange of activities taking place between the earth's depths and the breadths of the heavens. See how the blossoming roses grow out of the earth, look at the particular way the rosebud pinches its petals so tightly together as to complement the ground of the earth, counter positioned to the central point of the earth as a mighty rose of light, permeated with divine thought gestures which need to wait until the rose unfolds its bud upwards. Every sleeping rosebud you empathise with the waiting, creating, living light rose in the earthly depths. So it is with all plants. Look at the green cover of plants over the earth and experience that which sprouts out of the earth as green, in the depths of the earth, as quite light-filled but permeated with deep violet, which appears in the world, weaving through it with life. Then you have something which I have said to you: 'I may only call myself a human-being, when I have explored myself in the earth's depths.'

Third Lecture

So, the feeling must be reached towards becoming worthy through such meditative penetration, through the conquering of this first step, for the word "human-being" to be used for people. When one takes what the profane person takes as obvious, as a level hovering high above and think one can only reach this level by climbing up to it; through humbling yourself three times more than an ordinary person, becoming three times more humble than an ordinary person believes himself to be, then one is only starting to sense oneself gradually approaching the calling of a priest.

When one has gradually in such a way led oneself to reach the first step, then one takes on the second step which lets us look into the infinite widths of the worlds and one says to oneself at the present moment: Oh, how trivial this world has become, where humanity has only developed trivial images of the wide world. Yes truly, wiser than the wisest student was Stifter's grandmother who was asked about the evening red glow and answered it was the mantle of God's mother, which is hung out in the heaven to be aired. This naive, picturesque imagination is in contrast to scientific knowledge much wiser, much wiser than the most learned astronomy.

This one must be able to absorb: To actually see the shining stars in wide space, stars with essentially the eyes of divine spiritual beings who glance down at us, children of the earth, while their spiritual hands reach out to us, while our spiritual hands reach up to their spiritual hands because we were with them before we came down to an earthly existence. The gods look after us out of space, out of the heights above worlds, in order to explore how we feel towards their predisposition while our spiritual hands reached their spiritual hands. When we are able to possibly develop many imaginations of the heights and become more and more empathic, how the being of humanity originate out of the heights, towards which it needs to climb up once again, then we will be able to come one step closer to earn the right to, as people, call ourselves 'human beings.'

The word 'human-being' must first be dipped into the depths of the earth, as I have indicated, so that its absorption during this immersion becomes part of our minds and enable us to say: We understand this. Now this word 'human-being' need to rise up with the mists into the heights and give us the feeling that it will come again in the falling rain, when the word "human-being" will carry within itself the possibility of learning to understand it. We really must initially be clear about everything which works between the depths of the earth and the heavenly heights. In a lively way we must follow the haze rising from woods and mountains. We must not believe that the haze is rising from an area which belongs to the earth. We must develop every kind of modesty towards those people who see in a drop the dragon rising in a thermometer or a barometer, to facilitate measurements. The tendency is to immerse everything in earthly images only. We must reach a point where we can say: 'How foolish to believe thunder develops out of the friction between clouds; clouds consist of water as every child knows, all moisture is completely kept away from a glass rod if electricity is to be created.' — Naturally this foolishness comes to the fore when a person tries to experience something in the heights of heaven which he experiences on earth for he has descended down from the heavenly heights and now he needs to feel related to it again before he can truly call himself a human-being. We must clearly understand that while the fog rises out of the mountains and forests, where water is somewhat different than it is on earth, in regions where water itself becomes spiritualised, it is 'de-watered' and goes through spiritual processes so that it can materialise once again until it descends again as rain out of spiritual spheres. We must know that if we rise up into such regions then we need to be familiar with these regions of our origination, out of which we descended from in a previous existence. We need to know that

Third Lecture

lightening is something which rules and weaves in spiritual regions and take the imagination of ancient times, where lightening was the arrow of the Gods, as an imagination far more wise than we can ever make today.

In total stillness we must be able to develop such meditative imaginations in the depths of our minds, enabling us to be the leaders turning a completely de-spiritualised world culture towards the Spirit. When we turn towards the hard earth, we must also turn towards the gentle, flowing water, combining with one another in the depths, right into the most concentrated minute matter, which expands in the heights and must atomise, then coalesce to become rain again in their descent to earth. We must discover all the secrets of water, everything relating to water and draw it all together in our minds. We must meditate over it, we must ask ourselves: 'How does the sun's warmth come out of the world expanse during summer and into the earth to enable plants to bear fruit which turn ripe? How does this warmth of the sun sink into the earth to enable the farmer to entrust his seeds in the earth's warmth during winter?' At the end of Winter, it is this warmth which expands again into the vastness of existence. This warmth, found in all areas of existence, working in all cosmic undertakings, is a communion of the opposites between the heavenly heights and the earthly depths. As human-beings we originate from both. We must fathom the earth's depths before we can enter into the world's expanse.

By increasingly entering into such meditations, we come to a kind of feeling, a mindfulness, towards the second step, which gives us the right to apply the word 'human-being' to ourselves. We must achieve an awareness that all languages can only be provisional, until through the third step we have reached that union with the linguistic genius who actually speaks unconsciously within us while we, when we have made ourselves the tool of God's Word, only then need to have the right to apply the word 'human-being' to ourselves.

As a third step we must try and observe the world's expanse. This we can perceive when the rising and the setting sun becomes a reality in our minds. Similarly with the rising and sinking stars when we learn to understand the great journey of the sun chariot going through the world, then we are really able to recognise what the variations are between East and West, what is different from Southeast compared to Northwest and so on. This we can observe when we are able to say to ourselves: You as human-being may take five steps and so change your position on the earth's surface. For you to be able to do so, like the animal as well, is as a result of forces which draw from East to West in width and breadth, also working on you. You are also shaped out of the earth's depths. While the heights of heaven throw light on you from above and forms and enlivens you, you are all given the ability to be formed into beings able to walk on the earth's surface. The world's expanse you should sense and you *can* sense this by placing yourself in some distant landscape and experience the air as becoming something increasingly more real. In your immediate surroundings the air appears transparent to you, you don't see it; when you look at a mountain you can paint the air with it because it appears as dew on the surface; when you look at the air in the distance then you see the blue sky. Drenched with it you experience the beings of light as a feeling which becomes real because the experience is bound to actions of will. Thus you rise to the third step in your meditation which leads you to earn the right to name yourself a 'human-being.'

When you deepen this step in the secret of breathing, you start to understand what the air and the widths of the world are; what is working in the heights and depths and in the horizon and you admit: what permeates your breathing lives in the wide world — it is how the wide world experiences you — and it is this that you must sense in your breath. Further, you must sense in your breathing that an act of will is the basis of penetrating your entire being with the powerful impulses of breathing. You get an inkling of how the depths of the earth give material cohesion to your entire body which you transform according to thoughts given to you from the wide world. So they work together in the whole person:

> Depths of earth in your Physical

> World widths in your Astral

> Heavenly heights in your Etheric

Thus, you can feel entire cosmic dimensions in yourself. You can sense when you enter with your feeling into the diamond hard earth how you are a sleeping being. You can feel, when you raise your gaze to the heavenly heights, you are snatched from sleep and become a dreaming being. Yet you can also feel how you are a being who is awake in the width of the world. Gradually you learn to recognise the comic human in the earthly human-being.

In this way you learn to recognise how the human-being is actually formed by God out of the entire cosmos, placed by God on earth. Thus, you sense the threefold positioning in the cosmos. This is how you learn to feel how the Father God works out of the earth, whose lively activity must preferably be looked for in the past because what has remained is the firm ground on which we stand, the fixed forms repeated in the world, all that has remained appears to us in fixed images. By meditating with our mind sunk into the earthly depths we hear the words of the Father God sounding up to us. Out of the heavenly heights we hear how the presence of God speaks to us but the words are more profound and more complicated that human speech. God has descended from the heavens down to earth and had to go through the

Mystery of Golgotha to allow heavenly speech to penetrate our words. The actual communion of the earthly with the heavenly we can depict in the rising water vapour, in the rain which falls down again, in the rising and again descending warmth of the world. When we allow that to work in us it will permeate us with spirit, and we will sense the presence of Christ in those who we feel are under the influence of the heavenly heights. When we penetrate into our breath as coming out of the widths of space and we humbly link our feeling to what happens at every instant, when we in our physicality, ruled by the forces of earthly depths, feel formed and shaped under the leadership of Christ Jesus out of the heavenly heights then we come to really experience, and are permeated by, the activity of the Holy Ghost as the fulfilment of the Trinity and thus out of this our meditation could be:

The Father God has given me the strength which lies in my material existence, as solidified Spirit.

The Son God is always the heavenly which lives in me, which works and weaves like a watery cosmic existence, which is a symbol, an image of it. I sense Christ-God in all my weaving and living, in all which has made me from a child to an adult, in all which grows in me daily and needs to perish again, enabling me to be an earthling through my becoming.

I feel the Spirit God carry into the future that which Christ Jesus has become in us, in the past.

You see, when you meditate like this on the content born out of a word, a word previously only used provisionally, then you have earned the right to call a person a 'human-being.' We must begin by developing reverence towards the genius of speech because through such a meditation real reverence is cultivated. Our starting point must not be to refer to the outer impression of the human form only but as a human-being created by God, as a thought from God, as a God-filled human-being, when we speak.

Third Lecture

When we prepare ourselves as we have through our meditation on a word such as 'human-being,' then the impulse is born for these three steps to be applied to some other words and for the human speech on earth to be implemented in this way. The genius of speech will teach us how we can become living tools for the Word of God when we allow the congregation to experience this Word of God. The Word of God is always there, and what we are doing, is but a moment's experience of the continuous spiritual cosmic weaving Word of God. In the very first beginnings, the word existed. In ancient beginnings, it was already divine. When we are however not in the position to sense the holiness in the words 'human-being' for the people, then our approach is not right, we do not have dignity to also express the first words of the St John's Gospel in the correct way. The priest today has not yet come so far as to be able to say these words in this way.

In our time the primary importance for priests, if they continue in their calling, is to further such things. What has actually been left over from the ancient words revealed from the holy heights above the earth? What has remained from the words such as "Deus," "Christus," "Spiritum"? Earthly sounds they now are, hardened by dogma. The truth within words needs to be awakened in us, the truth of these words must live in us. We may not neglect anything which will still make it possible for the old, hardened and therefore dogmatic words to become alive again within us. We may no longer turn and twist in the way it was done with God's words in past times in which the Catholic Church extracted the Mystery of the Mass.

In the Old Mysteries priests were far more humble than those of today, when they are like I have just described them. The priest of old said to himself he couldn't be a priest if he was just as he was. As a result, before he was allowed to speak, those things were performed in which the last remainder of incense was still held. As a result of the sensing, which has come to its right in our

The Essence of the Active Word

Consecration of Man ritual, there is indicated that in the Mysteries of old, outer substances were used to shift the consciousness of the priests. This resulted in them feeling shifted out of their bodies and enchanted by the genius of speech, taking them to the higher Genius so that the priest of old, out of his body, experienced the Being of God. No priest was of the opinion that he could move his tongue when he expressed the Word of God; he knew he had to first go out of himself and allow his tongue to be moved from outside. We can no longer do this today and nor should we try. We should through inner spiritual means, with internalized feeling and will work towards the understanding of the foregoing, when we can call ourselves 'human-beings.'

Just consider, my dear friends, what the Act of Consecration will become under your handling when you start from today taking these things I've spoken about into your priest meditations. These things can also just gradually be taken in by us. Mankind has distanced itself from the divine and must find its way back again. We have absorbed the Act of Consecration into the Christian Movement for Religious Renewal like religious artists. Today we have come to the point where what can only be accepted like a religious art must be taken up in such a way that we are in the position to make it into a lively organism, in order for the Act of Consecration to become really alive and in this way be experienced within the Christian Community as ever new at each fulfilment of the ritual, just like the physical body experiences something new each time it takes in nourishment.

My dear friends, take this into your souls: the Act of Consecration is to become alive. Through this you will earn the right to place yourselves in the earth's becoming and through the Act of Consecration be present within the earth's becoming. Then may you express the following truth: If this Act of Consecration is not performed then the earth will waste away and remain without nourishment. It would be just as if no plants would grow. Plants grow in the physical world; the Act of Consecration of Man must grow in the spiritual realm. If it was not enacted there on this higher level, it would be the same as if on the lower level of the physical earth no plants would grow. A human-being only has the right to say this when he or she succeeds in continuously enlivening the Act of Consecration so that this self-expressed word 'human-being' has been achieved in the correct manner and being and weaving, within the earthly existence, through achieving the three steps of inner soul development.

Only then, my dear friends, when you have experienced it in this sensitive way can you really place yourself in the right way in our present time. According to your need to gather again after a certain time, I may say this to you, because it belongs to the entire development of the Christian Community. Thus, you have taken something full of life into yourselves which can work in an enlivening way in yourselves. I wish that today's words are taken in all seriousness, in the right way.

Translator's note: "Mensch" has no English equivalent. Collins Dictionary considers mensch used in English as "a well-meaning person." Reverso suggests 'human,' 'person' and 'man.' Google adds 'individual' to this list. The word 'human' is seen in contrast to 'animal' or 'robot.' To translate "Mensch" as 'human-being' is not quite correct, nor is 'individuality' — the latter indicating a person being different from others in some way. "Mensch" has a humane as well as individual character, so the best solution is using the expression "human-being" in this translation. As "the Word" is under examination, a hyphen is an attempt at forming a single inseparable concept.

The Essence of the Active Word

Fourth Lecture

Stuttgart, 14 July 1923

Yes, my dear friends, I would like to supplement what I said yesterday. I wanted to offer it then already, but time was too short. This occasion gives us the opportunity to refer to our relationship we need to gradually re-establish with the Bible. The Bible, namely the New Testament, is a document which we must learn to grasp as a supersensible revelation, not in a dogmatic sense but through arriving at knowledge which indicates that religious documents originating up to about the time 4 AD were not only of human origin but were poured into the consciousness of humanity; knowledge which could not have come out of humanity. I would like to mention that you only need to bring humanity up to this point while a kind of instinctive atavistic consciousness still existed, presenting the most manifold images depicting the highest spiritual things and processes, yet these images were not conceptualised in human consciousness.

So, it has come about that right at the time when intellectualism has become authoritative, religious documents are misunderstood in many areas. They are approached with intellectual thinking and basically it is quite natural that even with much goodwill, misunderstandings come to the fore. Thus, it has happened that when today's presented texts are transcribed into a common language, they do not represent the original documents because a national language has an intellectual basis which is alien to the original elements in which the religious documents were embodied.

When religious documents, particularly the New Testament,

are referred back to in its original language, it also becomes apparent that this original language can no longer be experienced in an adequate way in the constitution of souls of today. Actually, a kind of untruthful element enters into the understanding of ancient religious knowledge, also the New Testament. It is hopeless to think that translations done up to now can somehow be improved continually, because it must firstly involve finding the preconditions which will enable a kind of reawakening of ancient spirituality with the purpose of really understanding religious documents. This we can do, this everyone can basically do, if the trouble is taken to apply researchable spiritual scientific facts to, let's say, the New Testament.

I would like to give a small example and that from one of the most important places in the New Testament. I would like to stress from the start that representations in the New Testament are connected to a historic fact; the depiction in the New Testament can only be understood when it is very clear that the fact of the Mystery of Golgotha is placed within the rest of humanity's evolution, but as a fact which falls outside the rest of humanity's laws. The Mystery of Golgotha is a totally singular event and for its understanding should not be considered out of historical foundations, but it should be grasped out of itself. Only when you take — I would like to call it super-historical fact — this cosmic fact in relationship with scientific spiritual knowledge about the development of humanity, only then can you actually start understanding the deep sense of the words and the sentence formation of the New Testament. If you don't do this, a far too strong trivial tone enters into the New Testament. We can remind ourselves of various impulses towards a possible understanding of the Bible where absolutely no preparatory understanding is regarded necessary and that it should simply be taken in a naive, primitive manner. You need to remind yourself of this fact in order to judge how strong the reluctance is to perceive the New Testament in its total profundity.

Fourth Lecture

Just consider, my dear friends, that the Mystery of Golgotha, taken in its right sense, was fulfilled for the earth as a specific act of grace out of higher spiritual worlds at a specific time when a certain part of humanity was passing over from a previous state of consciousness to the next one. At the time of the Mystery of Golgotha the evolution of humanity's becoming in earthly life reached up to an inner ego reality. The "I" gradually unfolded at the same time as the Mystery of Golgotha. We may not look for the connection between these two facts, whether causal or just as a connection. We may only consider it a connection when it is compared with one seeing something happening and something is done towards it out of free will. The Mystery of Golgotha appears as a cosmic fact of free will which has come about within the development of humanity in such a way, that the ego consciousness is awakened. Now, you know the remainder of the important facts which are linked to the appearance of the ego consciousness. Something extraordinary may be added to this. It is necessary to know that with the embodiment of the ego consciousness in evolution there was a condition where people looked up at every opportunity of their conscious lives to gods, or — where monotheism existed — to that God who has remained as an image of the Father God. As long as we stand in the imagination of the Father God, the imagination is fulfilled so that we can say: 'When a human being is aware of his ego nature then he feels that within his ego is the inner working of the Father God in his soul.' The Father God distils in a certain way a drop of his own Being which remains connected to the entire spiritual sea of the Father God, to the beings of individuals and every person can say to himself: 'The Father God is alive in me, the abundance of the Father God lives in me.' However, the entire humanity is permeated with the being of the Father God. Experiencing all of this at present is to say to yourself: 'I am!' That is: 'The Father God is in me.' — To live in this way in present times is becoming increasingly impossible. You must come to your own "I" via your own consciousness which makes it a product of yourself. This production of the individual "I" is in connection with the entire cosmic-spiritual world only possible when individuals identify themselves with Christ, thus with the Son of God.

What can be said about the relationship between people blessed by Christ and people who have not been enriched by Christ? Upon looking back at the consciousness of unblessed mankind, therefore the individual being of their souls, can you say: 'I am the only one who has been blessed with an "I"?' — No, the soul could only say: 'Within me the Father God lives and because He lives in me it enables me to say "I" to myself.' — People had not been completely individualised, the individual was a child of God, but as if the child was still connected to God by an umbilical cord. What the soul could have when it was aware of this divine capacity, it could have no more, later on. The Christ-blessed humanity acquired it in such a way that each single soul could take up their "I" out of this divine substance.

In this way the Christ-blessed people were able to take their own "I" out of the substance of their individual soul being.

Thus, the Christ brought the same as what the Father God had given humanity on earth, but He brought it in a new way in order for every individual to find a connection to the ego being born within. Thus, the Christ could say to humanity: 'I bring to you what you are used to recognise out of the Logos, but I bring it in a new way. I bring it to you through what the Father God has given to me, what He had given directly to you before, but for another state of consciousness. As his messenger I bring this treasure from the Father God to you, to each independent consciousness of yours, to every single individual. I don't want to just make you into some kind of member of the whole cosmos, I will by virtue of the full authority given to me by the Father God

Fourth Lecture

make each single one of you, if you want to come, into an "I" filled person with a divine consciousness.'

That the manner in which the divine consciousness should come to people now in a different way to what it had been in earlier times, is because of the Mystery of Golgotha. Similarly, it also applies to the Words of the Gospels taking on quite a different sense as a result of the Mystery of Golgotha. It is for instance possible to refer back to the stages of evolution of humanity from the contents of the Our Father prayer. It doesn't refer to the contents in this case but that the Our Father comes across in a different and in a newer way to the "I" filled conscious soul even though given in the same words, in the same sentences. Penetrating this event with spiritual powers makes it possible again for us to research it ourselves. This fact brings us back to the original meaning of the Gospels. This original meaning must be revealed again today. Humanity should not be allowed to be fobbed off with misunderstandings of Gospels not taken from a lofty view. One should overcome the point of understanding the matter in such a way as to ask oneself: Can you, when you are quite honest in your soul, today still, discover meaning in the words of John 17, verse 1 to 9?

My dear friends, much can be said and repeated about this if you want to disregard the facts that a clear understanding can't really be found. In an artificial way (of the commentator) no meaning can be linked to these words. Only through belief can meaning be connected to them because nothing actual is touched when you have one these sentences (of some or other terrible translation) in front of you. By contrast when you make an attempt to empathise with the (original) texts in a word-for-word translation into your mother tongue (original text says "German" — translator note), then a deeper meaning comes into it. You should not allow, if you are honest with yourself, to say these words would be simplified and be comprehensible to every

55

ordinary human mind, through artificial comments. Actually, you realise the deeper meaning in the original and this fact must be your starting point.

Humanity today would prefer not to have to search for such deep meaning in the Gospels. One can't escape the fact that there is deeper meaning which we need to discover. We can't deny it. It would be a subjective fantasy to say: 'Don't interpret anything in the Gospels, simply remain with the contents.' That as such is the interpretation. When we go back to the meaning which is there on quite a mundane level then we could translate it in the following way:

> *After Jesus saved him, he lifted his eyes to heaven and said: Father, the hour has come, let your son be revealed so that he may reveal you, as You have given him power over all who have flesh, so that he may give everlasting life to them. This now is everlasting life, that You are recognised as the only true God and Jesus Christ as your emissary. I have revealed Your being on earth, to fulfil the work You have given to me. And now reveal me, Father, with the light of revelation which came through You to me before the world began. I have brought You into manifestation to humanity which You assigned to me out of the world. They were Yours and You gave them to me and they have remained fulfilled with Your Word. Thus, they can see that everything which You have given me comes from You. For the power of thought which You have given me, I have brought to them. You have linked yourself to them and seen how I come from You and that You have given them to me. I pray for each single individual, not for humanity in general, but for those you have given me, for they are yours, created by you.*

As I have said to you before, this entire version is nothing other, my dear friends, than the facts of humanity's evolution depicted within the Gospels. The precise truth in the Gospels can be found when you enter into the spiritual facts within them. With

Fourth Lecture

this, the kind of awareness develops, I might say, for the right light to be thrown on the words. Is it not true, it is certainly not my intention to utter some idle criticism when I say it is not possible to say the words: *"Father, the hour has come for You to reveal your son, so that Your son can reveal you."* If you are honest, you will admit this doesn't really say anything, even by trying to make it comprehensible through the human heart. In contrast the truth becomes obvious by taking the Greek Text which says: *"Father, the hour has come, reveal your son ..."* which asks the Father to reveal the Son. δοξα The is no statement, the δοξα is to reveal, to announce, to-bring-to-recognition, and thus it is meant: *"... so that your son is revealed out of You."* The mediation of the Father-contents through the power of the Son are expressed directly in these words in a naive idea. Earlier, humanity had the substance of the Father God within them, as described. Now the Father God has brought the Son to becoming the mediator for humanity. This is really written here and is no lie: *"... as You have given him power over all who have flesh ..."* The expression "flesh" (Fleisch) is difficult to translate here because it can be misunderstood in ordinary speech. In fact, it should say: *"... as You have given him power over all human physical bodies so that he can give everlasting life for those given to him."* — When one contemplates these facts, that the human body originally had the consciousness of being filled with God and thus earned everlasting life, you realise that while this power no longer fills the consciousness, the bodies can no longer reflect back the gift of everlasting life. This is why the Christ had to be sent to humanity. *'This now is everlasting life, that You are recognised as the only true God and Jesus Christ your emissary. I have revealed Your Being on earth, to fulfil the work You have given to me. And now reveal me, Father, with the light of revelation which came through You to me before the world began. I have brought You into manifestation for humanity which you assigned me out of the world. They were Yours and You gave them to me, and they have remained fulfilled with Your Word.'*

Christ Jesus has made it possible to stop the Word from dying and for the contents of the Father substance to remain in humanity. If the Mystery of Golgotha had not taken place, humanity would have forgotten about this content. The Father God would have been forgotten if the Son had not perpetuated the Fatherly content. *Thus, they have seen that everything which You have given me comes from You. For the power of thought which You have given me, I have brought to them. You have linked yourself to them and seen how I come from You and that You have given them to me. I pray for each single individual, not for humanity in general, but for those you have given me, for they are yours, created by you.*

I add here 'for humanity in general' instead of 'for the World'. This is no longer understood. This spiritual connectivity experience has just been referred to which at the time was an acceptable image: For them as individuals, not only for humanity in general.

In truth, the New Testament does not become less beautiful, magnificent and sublime through our understanding of its contents. This concerns your correct positioning in the present, in the spiritual life of the present, in a religious movement of the present to once again return to the reality contained in the Gospels. How often the request surfaces for the necessity to return again to original Christendom! It fails because nothing can be achieved by an attempt to grasp the Logos in its ancient meaning and then one repeatedly comforts oneself conveniently that the Gospels should be taken up as simple content. However, simple content would not fail if one would actually enter into what is written there. We may not forget, my dear friends, that words do essentially change in their feeling-value in the course of time. It is not possible simply to translate a word out of the ancient language lexicographically. Already today when one translates something

Fourth Lecture

lexicographically, the results are entirely different. This applies even more when translating historical events. It does not come down to directly taking the sentimental value attached to words of the present and applying this to ancient wording, but the task is to go back to the feeling within the contents of the *ancient* working. We can find examples of these facts everywhere in the New Testament where the Gospels were expressed in a time when revelation was given through grace from the spiritual cosmos to mankind which had not yet moved from the partially developed ego consciousness into the fully developed ego consciousness. All other facts need to be judged according to this basic fact. We may not remain fixed in an opinion and say that the earlier, the simple people emerging from the lowest levels could not understand the meaning in it. If the meaning of the Gospels is so simple to understand, we must reveal the other side of this wonderful fact: How were these simple people capable of relating such a profound meaning in the Gospels? — It is far more spiritual to say these simple people born from the folk could not have understood the meaning. Such a conclusion depends on another opinion.

I don't know if any of you — perhaps those of us who are older — have had this kind of experience of going with a loving heart among the country folk. You go there as an educated person feeling tremendously clever and you speak to the folk of what you've learnt. They don't understand you. Yet if you go along with them, you discover an unbelievable deep wisdom among these simple people which outshines anything you can offer out of yourself. The wisdom of naive people is actually deeper than that of educated people. The theory of simplicity among primitive people is an intellectual theory of educated people. For example, the meaning in some of Jakob Bohme's sentences could have been learnt from a herb gatherer forty years ago rather than in a university. This can't be denied. However faithfully an old text can be translated is something from which Professor Beckh can create a song for you, concerning Sanskrit in oriental texts. One will not be going too far by saying Indian philosophy becomes unrecognizable in translation, which for example was done by Professor Deußen (after the visit of Swami Viviknanda to Germany in 1896-translator note). If one wants to examine the original human contents of Deußen's translation, simply the straightforward word combination, you experience it as empty words in which no sense can be found at all. These things are of the utmost importance and are related to the deepest questions of our time. As a result, I do not want to hesitate to decide our future meeting in relation with this consideration, because I believe that it is necessary precisely at this time.

I hope you can experience it as the truth — what I mentioned yesterday — that for the Religious Movement the Act of Consecration becomes the deepest and most everlasting fact which is not merely rich in imagery but that it must become alive and remain capable of becoming ever new and more rich. I hope that we can continue with our working together in this lively unfolding way with which we have started with so much hope.

Werner Klein expressed in closing the wish of the good will remaining so powerfully in the work that in a year's time another meeting will be held where they could ask Dr Steiner's advice.

Rudolf Steiner: We wish for this as well and will hold this in our hearts.

Directory Of Rudolf Steiner's Original Manuscripts

(with Archive Numbers)

It approaches me in my work on earth (December 31, 1922)
  NB 21   GA 219
  (Discussed on July 12, 1923. Facsimile in the 6th edition
  (1994) of the volume "[The Relationship of the Stars to
  Man, and Man to the Stars](#)", GA 219)
John 17, 1-9: After Jesus had spoken these things
  (discussed on July 14, 1923)
  NZ 3479   63-64
Epistles:
  Advent (given October 1923)
    NZ 3547-3549   65-70
  Christmas (given December 1922)
    NZ 3585-3588   71-76
  Epiphany (given January 1924)
    NZ 3550-3551   77-80
  Passion week, Char week, Easter days (February 1923)
    NZ 3571-3577   81-92
  Ascension and Pentecost (given September 1923)
    NZ 3559-3561   92-99
  St. John's Day (given June 12, 1924)
    NZ 3552-3554   100-102
  Michaelmas (given September 1923
    NZ 3559-3561   103-106
Children's funeral (given March 1923)
  NZ 3578-3584   107-114
Consecration of the dead (given March 1923)
  NZ 3523-3524   115-116
Marriage (given spring 1922 to Pastor Wilhelm Ruhtenberg)
  NZ 4964-4969   117-122

The Essence of the Active Word

John 17, 1-9: After Jesus Had Spoken …
(discussed on 14 July 1923)
NZ 3479
Manuscripts 1-2

Nachdem
Es hatte Jesus dieses ~~Wort~~ geredet hatte, erhob er seine Augen ~~zu~~ zum Himmel und
sagte = Vater, die Stunde ist gekommen, ~~offenbare~~ (deinen Sohn, auf das
dein Sohn ~~dich~~ offenbare ; (wie ~~hast~~) ihm Macht über alles Fleisch gegeben hast,
damit er den Ihm zu eigen gegebenen das dauernde Leben gebe. Das aber
ist das dauernde Leben, dass sie Dich als den einzig wahren Gott erkennen
und ~~dessen, den du gesandt~~ Jesus Christus als den & abgesandten. Ich habe
Dich auf Erden geoffenbaret ~~wie~~, ~~ich vollendeten~~ Ziele zu bringen das Werk,
das Du mir zu thun aufgeleit hast. Und nun, offenbare mich, Vater,
und der Offenbarung, die mir dein Ding war), ehe die Welt bestand,
Ich habe zu jeder Erscheinung gebraucht für die Menschen, welche Du mir
aus der Welt zugeteilt hast. Dein waren sie und du gabst sie mir, und
~~sie~~ sie sind von Deinen Worten erfüllt geblieben.

The Essence of the Active Word

Epistles:
Advent
(October 1923)
NZ 3547-3549
Manuscripts 3-8

<u>Adventzeit</u> <u>Epistel</u>

Sinnend werden unsere Seelen,
Indem wir vor dem Altare stehen;
Die Menschen-Weihe-Handlung
Wird zur Geistes-Ahnung;
Der Seelenschleier legt sich
Vor das Schauen des Geistes-Auges.
Es wird still vor dem Geistes-Auge,
Es wird hörbar in dem Seelengründe
Das Walten des Welt-Vatergrundes
Die Weltenruhe in uns

The Essence of the Active Word

Erfüllet sich mit dem hörbaren Walten
Das verheissend spricht
Im hoffenden Menschenherzen.
Göttliche Weltenmacht,
Die DU glänzest im Sonnenwagen,
Die DU leuchtest im Farbenbogen,
Der den Himmel umspannt:
DU sprichst im Seelen-Innern.
Doch DEIN sprechen
Ist nicht gegenwärt'ges Tönen,
Ist Zukunftwort, das leise

In die Gegenwart sich trägt.
Ein „Werde" spricht es
Und ahnend erweckt es
Das Bild des Menschen = Werdens
In dem Gottes Werden sich birgt
Gottes - Werden, das in Gnade
Unsere Irrtümer huldvoll
In die eigne göttliche Seele
Erlösend bergen will.

The Essence of the Active Word

Empfinden kann unser Herz,
Das Heil, das im Weltenschoose
Verheissend keimt,
Das im Seelen-Innern
Der Welten-Geheimnisse
Menschen-tröstend
Prophetisch in dunkler Weltennacht
Spricht, kündend sein Wirken
Im Erdenreich.
Wirkend im Erdenreich,
Das prophetisch spricht

Im Glänzen des Sonnenwagens
Im Leuchten des Farbenbogens,
Da den Himmel einspannt.

Als Evangelium lesen: Luk. 282. (21) Es werden Zeichen sein -
Dann einfügen : (von der Ätherwelt aus, nach dem Chr. i. euch)

Dämmerung waltet
Im Umkreis des All's
Des Glänzen des Sonnenwagens,
Das Leuchten des Farbenbogens,
Der den Himmel einspannt.

The Essence of the Active Word

Sie dämmern in die Weiten;
Ahnung wird aus Dämmerung,
Sonnenwagen = Leuchten
Farbenbogen = Glänzen
Erzeugen sich neu;
Heil unserem Ahnen,
Heil unserem Hoffen,
Heil dem lichtgeborenen
Heil dem Farbengetragnen
Ewigen, göttlich = waltenden
    Worte.

Christmas
(December 1922)
NZ 3585-3588
Manu scripts 9-16

Epistel der ersten Messe:

In die Erden-Nacht

In die Sinnen-Finsternis

Strahlet des Geistes

Heilendes Gnadenlicht

Es erstrahlet uns

Wenn wir wandeln

Leibbefreit im Geisterland

Nachdem das Herz in uns

Es gefühlet im ahnenden Gebete

The Essence of the Active Word

Epistel der zweiten Messe:

Väterlicher Weltengrund:
Unsere Seele
Erfühlet das Nahen
Des heilenden Schöpferwortes;
Segnend erströme uns seine Kraft,
Auf dass es berühre unsere sprechende Lippe,
Und erwärme unser sprachetragendes Blut
Und erstarke unser geistergebenes Wollen
Durch alle künftigen Zeitenkreise.

Epistel der dritten Messe:

Christus, des väterlichen Weltengrundes
Offenbarender Schöpfergeist
Hat den Erdenleib erkoren,
In dem er wohnen mag,
Zu lösen den Menschen
Von trügendem Scheinlicht,
Zu lösen den Menschen
Von würdeloser Sinnensucht
In allen künftigen Zeitenkreisen.

Nach dem Staffelgebet (bei allen drei Messen)

Mitte des Altars, Gesicht gegen die Gläubigen,

Erkennet es:
Der Christus ist im Erdenreich erschienen:
Schauet in ihm:
Den Heilbringer der Erdenmenschen
Durch ist ist offenbar worden:
Der Vatergrund alles Seins.

Bei der dritten Messe:
                              nach dem Opf..
Zur Weihnacht vor dem Canon einzuschalten:
(Mitte des Altars, gebügt dem Altar zugewendet)

Väterlichen Urgrund alles Seins

Indem durch das Wort, das im Erdenleib gelebt

Unserem geistigen Schauen das Licht Deiner klaren Leuchtkraft sich entschlossen hat,

Auf dass wir das Göttliche

Sichtbarlich erkennen

Und dadurch für das Unfassbare unsere Liebe sich entzünde.

The Essence of the Active Word

Stimmen wir ein
In den Urgesang
Der Engel, Erzengel, der Urkräfte, der Offenbaren, der Weltenkräfte,
der Weltenlenker, der Throne, der Cherubim und
Seraphim

Der ertönt, auf dass Du offenbar werdest;

Und durch alle Zeitenläufe

Ertöne es: Seilwirkendes ist durch Dich.

Epiphany
(January 1924)
NZ 3550-3551
Manuscripts 17-20

Epiphanie

Epistel:

Aus den Weltenweiten
Erschien der Gnaden-Stern
Zu fügen Herz-Erwärmung
Zur Geist-Erleuchtung
Im Menschenwesen.

In das Gnaden-Licht
In des Christus-Sternes
Begnadenden Strahl
Möchten unsere Seelen
Ergeben dem ew'gen Vaterwillen,

The Essence of the Active Word

In Demut treten.

Vollbracht sei

Die heil'ge Weihe-Handlung

Im Seelen-Aufblick

Zu dem Sterne

Der die Engel rief

Zu Künden

Den Welt-Weisen

Des Welten-Lichtes

Gnade-Erscheinung.

Unser's Gebetes Herzenslicht
Treffe sehnsüchtig
Des Gnadesternes Weltenlicht.
Und Leben im Christus
Erstehe im Menschen-Innern
Wenn in's Seelen-Auge dringt
Des Gnadesternes Geistes-Strahl.

Als Evangelium: Math. Cap. 2.
Nach der Evang.-Lesung, von der Altar-Mitte, gegen die
entsprech. Form (Chr. i. E.) eingerahmt:

THE ESSENCE OF THE ACTIVE WORD

Es kündigten die Geistes-Welten
Sternstrahlend
Den suchenden
Menschenseelen
Des Heiles rechten Weg;
Es mögen finden die Menschen-Seelen
Herz=Liebe=strahlend
Den weg-weisenden
Welten-Gnade-Stern
Im göttlich-warmen
Heiles-Leuchten-

Passion Week, Holy Week, Easter
(February 1923)
NZ 3571-3577
Manuscripts 21-34

Epistel der Passionswochen.

9 Wochen vor der Charwoche.

O Mensch : es ist leer
die Stätte deines Herzens,
Du hast verloren
Den Geist, der dich wecket
Sehnsucht nach des Geistes
    Erweckung
Wellt im Blute der
Entbehrung durch des Geistes
    Verlust
Wogt im Atem dir —
Trauernde Erwartung
Ist deines Bewusstseins
    Anteil.

In der ganzen Passionszeit bis einschl. Karsamstag (4 Wochen)
nach dem Evangelium vor der Opferung.
Der Celebrierende in der Altarmitte
Spricht gegen den Altar =

Siehe o Geist

Der Weltenfernen

Und der Erdennäh

Nicht des Bösen

Stachel im Herzen

Das Erdenmenschen
Sicht seiner Schwäche
Versuchende Macht –
Mein Ich liegt
Klagend am Boden
Erhebe es, o Geist
Der Weltenfernen
Und der Erdennähe.

The Essence of the Active Word

Epistel in der Charwoche:

O Mensch, es brennet
die Stätte deines Herzens
Du lebst in dem kalten
geistverlass'nen
Erdenhause —
Betrübnis rieselt
Dir im Blute
Hoffnung allein
Strömt dir im Atem —

Epistel der Ostertage (Sonntag Beginn:) bis zu Pfingsten.

Das Grab ist leer
Das Herz ist voll
Wärme wandelt
Des Herzens Schlag
In frohlockende
Heilende Kraft
Deines Blutes Weben
Ist Erfüllung
Deines Atems Wogen
Ist Geistestrost
Der Tröster deines Erdenjesus
Wandelt im geiste
Vor dir.

The Essence of the Active Word

Vom Ostersonntag ab – ~~es~~ vor dem Evangelienlesen
Das Buch bleibt auf dem rechten Altarseite liegen
Der Celebrierende steht in der Mitte des Altars
mit dem Gesicht zum Altar die Arme hoch
etwas nach oben gehalten und ausgebreitet =

Es lobet mein Herz

Den Gottesgeist

Es jubelt mein Geist

Den Todbesieger

Jubel ist meines Atems
Strömende Kraft
Gnade ist meines Blutes
Lebendige Macht —
[Sich zu den Gläubigen wendend]
Euer Wort dringe
Geist-erweckt
Aus eurem Munde
Christus ist euch
Als Erdensinn erstanden.

THE ESSENCE OF THE ACTIVE WORD

Vom Ostersonntag an nach dem Evang. vor der Opferung
Der Chlebrierende in der Altarmitte, Gesicht zum Altar –
hocherhobene Hände, etwas ausgebreitet:

(gesprochen mit grosser Hingebung und Wärme)

Es ~~jubilieren~~ frohlocket
In Wonne
Der Kreis der Erdentief
Es lebt
In geisteleuchtender
Sonnenkraft
Der Erde Atem

Christus ist eingezogen
In des Menschen
Frohlockenden
Lebenspuls
Der Mensch findet
In der Wonne
Seiner hingebenden Seele =
Was in Kraft erstanden
Aus Todesketten
Was im Lichte neugeboren
In Christi Leben
Was heilet das Ich
In den Seelengründen.

The Essence of the Active Word

Es lebet die Seele,
die tot war
Es leuchtet das Ich
das finster war
Es kraftet der Geist
der verschlossen war.
Es öffnet sich
der Seele Grab
Zum Altar wird
der Seele Grab

Christus opfert
Am Seelen-Altar
Im Menschen=Geisteslichte
Den Weltenfernen
Der Erdennähe
Jetzt und nach allen Zeitenkreisen.

The Essence of the Active Word

Ascension and Pentecost
(September 1923)
NZ 3559-3561
Manuscripts 34-42

Chi Himmelfahrt Epistel: In demselben Rahmen und an
                            der Stelle des Stoff-Geb.

(Himmelfahrt bis Pfingsten)

Göttlicher Vatergrund,

Der Du walltest

Unter allen Wesen;

Du hast JHN gesandt,

Und Er hat Seine Sendung bekräftiget

Durch Lehre, Leiden

Durch Tod und Todes-Sieg;

Er lebet im Erdensein,
Verklärend das Erdensein
Mit Himmelssein;
Wir schauen mit Herzensseherkraft
Seine Erhöhung
Zum Himmelssein für das Erdensein.

Er wohne bei uns,
Indem Er wohnet bei Dir.
Mit Seiner Kraft
In unseren Seelen
Wollen wir verrichten
Die Weihe-Handlung
Aufblickend zu IHM.

2

Als Evangelium soll gelesen werden:

Joh. 16: Bittet, aus dem Herzen
So wird einem Herzen gegeben. (vorschriftlich von Vers 22

(auf Credo, nicht nur Faust)

Zwischen Evang. und Offertorium:

Es offenbaret sich
Christi Seelenkraft
In den Höhen,
Denen Er einverleibt
Das Erdensein.
Unsere Seelenaugen

Schauen Ihn
Im Wolkenschein,
Segen spendend
Dem Erdensein.
Darob lobpreisen Ihn
Unsere Herzen
Und unser Preisgesang
Folge Seinen Spuren,
Auf dass wir seien
Die sich zu Ihm bekennen
Durch alle Zeitenkreise.

Pfingsten: [sketch/notes]

Epistel:

Christus sendet
In unsere Seelen
Des Vatergründes Geist,
Der da heilet
Als der Weltenarzt
Der Seelen Schwachheit
Und der Menschheit Gebreste.
Der Heilbringende Geist
Walte in dem Opferworte
Segnend die Opfertat,

Die da wirket
In der Weihe-Handlung,
Die entstammet
Der Einsetzung Christi,
Die geschehe
In dem Lichte
Des Geistes
Der da heilet,
Was krank sich erweiset
Im Erdensein.

4.

Es wird als Evangelium gelesen:

Joh. 14: Wer mich wahrhaft liebt (wahrscheinlich vor Vers 23 an)
Offenbaret meinem Geist.   [may cresco] (aufgeführtes Läuten)

Zwischen Evang. und Offent.: [may cresco] (aufgeführtes Läuten)

Schauet die Flammen
Sie sind des Geistes Offenbarung.
Es flamme das Wort
Der Weihe-Handlung
Es flamme die Tat
Der Weihe-Handlung.

Die Flammen strahlen himmelwärts;
Sie erstrahlen aus Menschenherzen,
Die erfüllet von Christus
Ihr Wesen entzünden
In Lobesworte,
Das erfüllt vom Geiste,
Den Er herangezogen,
Dass Geistgeheilt
Menschen-Seelen
Gesund sich halten
Durch alle Erden-Zeitenkreise.

The Essence of the Active Word
St. John's Tide
(June 12, 1924)
NZ 3552-3554
Manuscripts 43-48

Joh. Ep.

Zu dem Vatergotte
Dem allwaltenden
Dem allsegnenden
Ströme unsrer Seelen
Fromm = ergebener
Herzwarmer Dank

In Aetherweiten wirket gnadestrahlend
Weltenlicht, in Fülle, in reifendem Glanze
Des Vatergottes allwaltende Kraft
Des Vatergottes allsegnende Macht

Sie wirken im flutenden Aetherlicht
Sie schaffen in lebender Wesenswelt
Sie reifen in der Welten-Mitte
Zur menschen = erlösenden Christus-Sonne.

In des Sonnengeistes Aetherstrahlen
Zogest Du, unser Erretter
In des Erdenfeldes schuldbeladne
Heilbedürft'ge Menschensaat.

Und der den Vatergeist
Im Umkreis seines Leibes
Demutvoll tragende

Joannes

Es sprach der Verkündigung
Heiltragendes, schuldbewusstes
   Flammenwort

Sein Gnadeahnendes
   Flammenwort
Es brenne in unsren Herzen
Verlangend nach Dir,
Der Du für uns Menschenfühlner
Das Leben aus dem Tod geboren

Auf dass wir leben
In reinen Aethersphären
Die schuldlosen nur tragen können
Auf den erglänzenden Geisteswellen.

Es offenbaret unseren Seelen
Der Licht = ersehnende
der Licht = erkennende
des Lichtes Gnadenstrahlung;
Es empfange unsere Seele
Den Lichtes = Spender
Den Lichtes = Schöpfer
In Lichtes = Liebe = Sinn.

The Essence of the Active Word

Nach der Opferung, vor der Wandlung:

Sonnenlicht = entflammtes
Weltenlicht = ergebenes
Du, der den Vatergeist
Im Umkreis seines Leibes
Demutvoll tragender
  Joannes
Heiles- Vor- Verkünder
Schaue auf des Altars
Menschensegnende Tat
Die wir vollbringen wollen

Durch Christi Segen
Der uns in Dir
Verkündet ist.

Michaelmas
(September 1923
NZ 3559-3561
Manuscripte 49-54

Epistel Mich.

Unsere Seelenaugen schauen, da wir
In dieser Stunde von dem Altar
Die Handlung der Menschenweihe
Im Herzen erleben wollen:
Das Antlitz dessen, der da ist
Selbst des Menschengottes Antlitz.
So stand er dereinst vor DEM,
Der Christus, den Menschenheiler
Aus Geistes-Höhen in Erdetiefen
Gnadevoll hat senden wollen.

So steht er in diesen Weltentagen
Hellstrahlend als Christi Antlitz
Als Hüter vor dem Weiheopfer.
Die Gewalten, die den Menschengeist
In Erdensclavenketten fesseln wollen,
Tritt er unter seine Füsse,
Die der Erdenschwere ledig sind.
Und aus Menschenherzen holet er
Die freie Kraft, die Irdisches
In Himmelshöhen läuternd
Und geisterempfangend tragen kann.

The Essence of the Active Word

Aus seinem Schein erkraftet Ernst,
Ernst, der vor Christi Milde
Das Menschenherz dem Licht bereitet.
Wer ihn schaute noch vor Jahren
Erblickt' die strenge Hand
Drohend nach des Drachen Kraft gestreckt.
Wer ihn heute schaut, wird gewahr
Wie die Strenge gegen Feindgewalt
Er für Augenblicke wandelt:
Und seine Hand zum Wink gestaltet,

Dem Menschen deutet: <u>Folge mir</u>.
Ich führe dich zum höhern Ahnen
Der Lebens-Todestat auf Golgatha.
Die fortwirkend im Erdenmenschen
In Zukunftszeiten schaffend
Dem Leben Licht bringen soll.
Dass im Erdenlichte nicht erlösche
Das Himmelslicht, das leuchten sollte
Wie vom Anbeginn, so jetzt
Und in allen Zeitenkreisen.

Als Evangelium das von der Königl. Hochzeit
Math. 22

Und dann einfügen: (von der Altarmitte aus) nach dem üblichen
Chr. ist auch — — —

 Der da steht vor dem Antlitz
 Dessen, der durch Golgatha
 Zu der Menschen Heilung gieng:
 Er führe uns in die Seelentiefen,
 Aus denen Christus seine Kraft
 Geisttragend in Menschenherzen
 Sendet, wenn Menschen fühlen
 In wahrer Heilessehnsucht
 Das Herzensfeuer recht entzündet.
 Der da stand vor dem Vatergott,
 Der da stehet vor dem Sohnesgotte:
 Zu IHM sollen wenden sich
 Unsere Herzen, dass der heilende Geist
 In uns wirke, wie vom Anbeginn,
 So jetzt und durch alle Zeitenkreise.

The Essence of the Active Word

Children's Funeral
(March, 1923)
NZ 3578-3584
Manuscripts 55-68

Beräucherung des Sarges.

Dann:

Zu Dir, o ewiger Weltengrund, o väterlicher Urheber
  aller sterblichen Menschenwesen
Erheben sich in Ergebung unsere leiderfüllten Seelen;
Du hast uns unser { Söhnchen / Töchterchen } zur Freude unserer
  Herzen aus Deinen lichtesreichen
In unser Erdenhaus geschickt;
Du hast es wieder entrückt in Deine Wohnung,
Ehe es der Menschen Erdenbahn mit eigner Kraft beschritten.
Wir stehen in Trauer und suchen Trost bei Dir,
Stärke unsere Seelen durch Deine Gotteskraft.
Unser(e) lieb(es) { Vorname } wird unserem Erdenauge
  unsichtbar sein,
Kräftige unser Geistesauge, auf das wir (ihn / sie)
  schauen unter denen,
  die bei Dir sind.
Deine Gnade sei Balsam unseres Leides.
Dein Hoffnungsstrahl falle auf unsere Thränen,
Er spricht zu uns:
Wir werden unsere(n) lieb(en) (Vorn.) bei Dir wiederfinden.

107

The Essence of the Active Word

2

Beräucherung des Sarges.

Dann wird etwas Asche auf den Sarg gestreut;
dann die Worte:

    Fallende Asche
Tote Erde ergreift den Tod
    des Lebenden
Lebende Erde wird einst quellen
    Aus des Lebenden
   Zerstäubendem
     Stoffe.

So bekennen wir:

   und des Rauches Kraft
  trage unser Bekenntnis
   In des Geistes
    Vaterreiche.

Hier folget die Trostansprache an Eltern Geschwister und
sonstige Leidtragende.

3.

Zu Dir, Christus in uns, liebeschenkender Menschentröster
  Unsterblicher Bruder der sterblichen Menschen.
Wenden sich hilfeflehend unsere leiderfüllten Seelen;
Du hast mit uns unser { Söhnchen / Töchterchen } mitfühlend als
  unsere Freude auf Erden empfangen
Und bist eingekehrt in sein Herz;
Du wirst es geleiten zum Geistestor,
Dass es finde den Weg ohne der Erdenreife Ende.
Wir stehen schmerzerfüllet und suchen Deine Kraft.

Wir fühlen Dich in unsrer trauernden Seele.
Unser(e) liebe(r) {Vorname} wird unseren Erdenwegen
  ferne sein,
Erwärme unseren Seelengrund, auf dass wir, (ihn/sie)
  erinnernd, (seine/ihre) Gegenwart
    fühlen in Deiner Gegenwart.
Deine Liebe sei die Stütze unseres verarmten Gemütes.
Dein Erdentod scheine auf unsere(n) Toten,
Er spricht zu uns:
Unseres(r) lieben {Vorname} Seele ist unter den in Christo Lebenden.

THE ESSENCE OF THE ACTIVE WORD

4

Wieder Beräucherung des Sarges.

dann werden einige Tropfen Wasser auf den Sarg gespritzt;
dann die Worte:

Weckendes Wasser
Wachstums Kräfte ergreifen die Seele
des Toten
Tote Kräfte werden ergeistet
In des Toten
Geistwärts dringenden
Seele.

So bekennen wir:

und des Rauches Kraft
vereine unser Bekenntnis
Mit des Christus
Kraft in uns.

Zu Dir, o Weltengeist, menschenseelenweckender
    Lichterstrahlender im Weltendunkel
Schauen wir hoffnungsvoll als verlassene Seelen;
Du wirst unser { Söhnchen / Töchterchen } geistweckend vom
    Erdenschlafe zum Geisteswachen führen,
Dir gehöret seine junge Erdenwesenheit;
Du wirst ein helles Flämmchen machen.
Aus ihm, dass sie leuchte im Weltengeisteoreich.
Wir stehen des Flämmchens entbehrend, das bei uns war,
Und wir suchen Deine Wärmeweckende Kraft.

Wir fühlen uns in Deinem grenzenlosen Hoffnungslicht.
Unser(e)n liebe(r) { Vorname } werden wir bei Dir wissen.
Erleuchte unser Seelenauge, dass es ahne
    { Ihn / Sie } in Deinen Strahlen
    In Deinem Geistes-Sternen-Reich.
Dein Licht leuchte über unsere ewige Gemeinschaft
    mit unserem lieben Toten,
Es spricht zu uns:
Unseres lieben (Vorname) Geist leuchtet sich und uns im Weltenlicht

6.

<u>Zuletzt noch einmal Beräucherung des Sarges</u>;
dann die Worte:

    Zur Erde fallet
  Was irdisch gestaltend
    Zum Geiste wallet
Was geistig erhaltend

  Ewiges Licht empfange
    Was Geist-geneigt
Ewiges Leben erlange
    Was Seele gezeigt

Im Entschwinden erhelle
    Die Geist-Seele sich
Im Verglimmen erquelle
    Der Seelen-Geist dich
Der als Vater trauend
    Und auch dich
Die als Mutter trauend
    Hier stehet
Erdenabschied nehmend
Geistesgruß von Eurem (Vorname)
  In Geistes-Reichen
    einst erhoffend.

Es kann, wenn die Umstände es nötig
machen das auf S. 1. u 2. vorgesehene
   im Hause
dann das auf S. 3–6 vorgesehene
   am Grabe, oder der Verbrennungsstätte
   celebriert werden.

Es kann auch alles auf S. 1–6 vorgesehene
   am Grabe oder der Verbrennungsstätte
   celebriert werden.

The Essence of the Active Word

Act of Consecration of the Dead
(March 1923)
NZ 3523-3524
Manuscripts 69-72

Die Menschenweihehandlung verläuft wie eine andere, nur wird als Evangelium gelesen:

    Mark. 16. Von der Auferstehung Jesu.

Nach der Kom. wird eingeschaltet:

    Mit dem Worte dieser Weihehandlung
    Senden unsere Seelen zu Dir
    O Christus, der Erwecker der Toten
    Die Gedanken die sie binden
    An die Seele unsere(s) teuren
    . . . . [Name]

    Mit dem Opfer, das wir
    Vollbringen dürften in Deinem Namen
    O Christus, der Führer der Seelen
    Senden unsere Seelen ihr Gebet
    Zu Dir, o Vatergott für unsere(n) teure(n)
    . . . . [Namen]

    Ih$_m^r$ leuchte das Licht der Räumesweiten
        In Geisteshöhen
    Ih$_m^r$ töne das Wort der Zeitenfernen
        In Seelenreiche

The Essence of the Active Word

Ihm lebe der Geist der Gottesoffenbarung
  In Gnadenwelten
Nimm {ihn/sie} auf in Deine Kraft
  O Vatergott
Aus Christi Hand
An der Todespforte
In Deine LebensKreise
Und führe zum Tage {ihn/sie}
Dem keine Nacht dunkelt
Weil ihm leuchtet
Das Licht, das da scheinet
Dem todlosen Leben.

Wedding Ceremony
(Spring of 1922 by Pastor Wilhelm Ruhtenberg)
NZ 4964-4969
Manuscripts 73-84

1.

Eine Art Tisch muß aufgestellt sein; auf demselben das Bild Christi.
Der Priester steht hinter dem Tisch; die zu Trauenden vor demselben
Der Priester spricht zunächst:

> Der Erden wirken
> Zu Geistes wirken
> In eigner Opfertat
> Wandelte,
> Stehe ich vor Euch:
> Vor dir [...... es wird der Name des Mannes genannt]
> Vor dir [...... es wird der Name der Frau genannt]

> Und vor Euch:
> Es werden die Trauzeugen genannt,
> Und vor allen,
> Die ihr Zeugen sein wollet,
> Dass [Name des Mannes] und [Name der Frau]
> Sich verbinden wollen
> Zum heiligen Ehebund.

× × ×

Und so frage ich dich (Name des Mannes):
Gedenkst du in jene Entschlüsse,
Mit denen du in der Geistwelt wandelst,

The Essence of the Active Word

2

Aufzunehmen
Des Lebens Gemeinsamkeit
Mit (Name der Frau).
 (Ja = Antwort des Mannes).
Und so frage ich dich (Name der Frau)
Gedenkst du in jene Entschlüsse,
Mit denen du in der Geistwelt wandelst
Aufzunehmen
Des Lebens Gemeinsamkeit
Mit (Name der Frau).
 (Ja = Antwort der Frau).
Nachdem [Name des Mannes] und [Name der Frau]
Durch ihres Wortes Kraft

Besiegelt haben
Ihres Lebens Gemeinschaft
Wendet sich zu Euch [den Zeugen] (Frau:)
Meiner Seele mahnendes Wort:
Eure Augen haben gesehen
Eure Ohren haben gehört:
Dass sich verbunden haben:
Dieses Mannes Geisteswille
Mit dieser Frau Seelengeist
Zur Lebens Gemeinsamkeit.
Nie darf aus euren Herzen schwinden
Nie darf aus eurer Seele sich verlieren
Bewusstsein dessen,
Was ihr gesehen, was ihr gehört.

Nie darf aus einem helfenden Willen
Sich hinwegstehlen
Lebendiger Beistand,
Den ihr damit gelobet
Dem Leben derer,
Die jetzt vor Euren Augen
Suchen das Tor
die Lebens Gemeinsamkeit.

.x.x

[Wenn Ringe gewechselt werden, so ist folgendes nunmehr zu vollziehen: Der Priester nimmt von der Hand des Mannes den Ring, den dieser bisher getragen hat (mit neuem eingravierten Namen); er legt ihn rechts von sich auf die Seite, wo die Frau steht; Dann nimmt er den entsprechen Ring von der Hand der Frau und legt ihn auf die Seite, wo der Mann steht; alles vor dem Bilde Christi.)

Dann spricht er:

Es rundet der Ring
Die Ecken des Lebens
Es fasset der Ring
Das Weben des Seins
Im Ringe lebet
Was aus dem Einzelnen
Sich schliesset zum Ganzen
Nimm hin
(Der Ring mit dem Namen des Mannes wird der Frau angesteckt.)
Den Ring
Des Kräfteflieszens

The Essence of the Active Word

4

Des Herzenbindens.
Ninon hin
(Der Ring mit dem Namen der Frau wird dem Manne angesteckt)
Den Ring
Des Kräfteschließens
Des Herzenbindens.
[Soll alles vollständig sein – namentlich sollte das folgende gemacht werden, wenn keine Ringe vorhanden sind], so folgt jetzt:
Es wird ein Stäbchen, das vorbereitet ist, an ein anderes durch einen Faden zu einem solchen X verbunden. Der Priester hält dieses Kreuz den zu Trauenden vor und spricht:

Es bindet sich
Was getrennt
Es leuchtet Geistgebundnes
In Seelenreichen
Zu des Lebens Gemeinsamkeit.
Es schaut eines Gottes Geist
Auf die Bindung
Des Getrennten
Zum Einenden
Du (Name des Mannes)
Leuchte ihr (Name der Frau)
Voraus mit dem Lichte
Das der Wieder-Erstandne (Priester weist nach dem Bilde Christi)
In deinem Geiste leuchten läßt;
Du (Name der Frau)
Folge ihm (Name des Mannes).

5

In dem Lichte,
Des der Wieder-Erstandene
In deiner Seele leuchten lässt.

× ʌ ×

Wenn man es angemessen findet, wird jetzt eine Traurede gehalten, deren Inhalt an die persönlichen Verhältnisse der zu Trauenden anklingt und die ausklingt in die Darstellung der Wichtigkeit des Augenblickes als Ausgangspunkt zweier Lebensschicksale.

× ʌ ×

Dann spricht der Priester:

Unter Christi Augen
In Geistes Webe-Wellen
Hat gesegnet

Des Wortes Kraft
Die Lebens Gemeinsamkeit;
Wir alle
Wollen bewahren
Die Siegeskraft
Des Wortes
Das gesegnet hat
Was Seelen wollen
In Wesenseinigkeit.
Über dem Schicksal
Von (Namen der beiden zu Trauenden)
Walte Gottes segnende Macht
Wirke Christi helfende Kraft
Leuchte Geistes strahlendes Licht.

The Essence of the Active Word

6.

Aus Gottes Welten
Kamen Eure Seelen;
Sie fanden sich
Im Erdensein —
Geisteslicht
 Leuchte
Ihrem Erdendenken
Seelenwärme
 ~~Ist~~ Strahle
Ihrem Erdenfühlen
Herzens innigkeit
 Krafte
Ihrem Erdenwollen

Zu ihrem Lebensglücke
Zu der ganzen Menschheit
 Heil und Glück.
 * *
 *

Es folgt als Segnende Geberde von seite des Priesters:
 Die beiden Arme werden nach oben gehoben,
 dann nach vorne im Ellenbogen gebeugt horizontal gestellen,
 dann über der Brust gekreuzt.

Dann gesprochen:
 So sei es. Amen.   Ende.
 * *
 *

NOTES

TEXT DOCUMENTS

The lectures were co-stenographed by Karl Lehofer. The printing of the lectures is based on the plain text transcription prepared by him. About the reliability of his transcripts see "Necessary Remarks on the quality of the transcripts" in Volume I of the series "Lectures and Courses on Christian-Religious Work," GA 342, pages 239-241. (see Appendix II)

NOTES ON THE TEXT

Works of Rudolf Steiner within the Gesamtausgabe (GA) are indicated in the notes with the bibliography number. See also the overview at the end of the volume.

Page

1 *Words ... [by Dr. Rittelmeyer]:* Friedrich Rittelmeyer (1872-1938), first arch-superintendent of the Christian Community.

"... how we were recently able to lead one of the oldest members of our anthroposophical movement, Hermann Linde, to cremation" [See Rudolf Steiner's address at the cremation of Hermann Linde in Basel, on June 29, 1923, contained in the volume "Our Dead", GA 261. (see Appendix I)]

Hermann Linde (1863-1923) was an art painter, since 1906 a member of the Theosophical or Anthroposophical Society. He was involved in the artistic design of the Munich performances of Rudolf Steiner's Mystery Dramas, was co-founder and 2nd chairman of the Johannesbau Association, and was actively involved in the artistic design of the first Goetheanum.

3 *"Thirteen linden"*: Epic by Friedrich Wilhelm Weber (1813-1894), Paderborn 1878, was circulated in over 200 editions at the time.

6 *the burning spark was laid*: The fire of the first Goetheanum on the night

The Essence of the Active Word

of New Year's Eve 1922/1923 was first noticed in the so-called "White Hall". in which the meetings of the founders of the Christian Community had taken place in September 1922.

13 *Ernst Curtius* (1814-1896), scholar of antiquity; his ceremonial addresses, held in Berlin as Professor Eloquentiae were published under the title "Antiquity and the Present," 3 volumes, Berlin 1875-1889.

17 *verdict of the astronomers*: The French astronomer and mathematician Pierre Simon de Laplace (1749-1827), asked by Napoleon why there was never any mention of God in his writings, answered: " Sire, I have never needed this hypothesis." (From: "The Dogmatists of Natural Science or Matter versus Spirit " by Hermann Klingebeil, Berlin 1906).

18 *Yesterday's lecture*: Lecture for members of the Anthroposophical Society, Stuttgart, July 11, 1923, contained in "The human soul in its connection with divine-spiritual individualities. The internalization of the annual festivals," GA 224.

26 *meeting of the delegates in February 1923*: In the lecture given in Dornach on March 3, 1923, the report on the assembly of delegates of February 27, 1923, contained in the volume "Anthroposophical Community Building," GA 257. See also "The Fateful Year 1923 in the History of the Anthroposophical Society," GA 259.

29 *As I have expressed it*: thinking is a communion of the human being. The realization of the idea in reality is the true communion of the human being. communion of man." Rudolf Steiner 1887 in the introduction to the 2. volume of the Kürschner edition of "Goethe's Natural Scientific Writings" in GA l, page 126.

30 *My lecture at that time*: the Dornach lecture of December 30, 1922, contained in the volume "The Relationship of the Starry World to Man and of Man to the Starry World. The spiritual communion of mankind" GA 219.

When one says that one cannot arrive at anthroposophical understanding [of the Christ] can be arrived at: In the version handed down by the stenographer this sentence is not quite comprehensible, it was therefore supplemented by the words "of the Christ." This addition is

NOTES

based on a letter from Professor Hans Wohlbold to Rudolf Steiner of December 2, 1922, in which he writes, that a priest in Munich had explained to the Christian Community "that one could that by staying away from the congregation, one is guilty of the fact that Christ cannot Christ cannot appear in the etheric body, and that those who are only anthroposophists the way to Christ remains closed to those who are only anthroposophists.

41 *Stifter's grandmother:* Ursula Stifter, née Kary (1756-1836). Adalbert Stifter has in the figure of her grandmother in his story "Das Heideorf" (Studies, Volume 1, 1844). Cf. also Rudolf Steiner's Dornach lecture of June 8, 1923, in "[The Artistic in its World Mission]()," GA 276.

60 *Hermann Beckh*: 1875-1937, Indologist and Sanskrit researcher, was professor for ancient languages, especially those of the Himalayan region, and had made many translations from ancient scriptures.

which for example was done by Professor Deußen, for example: Paul Deußen (1845-1919), a philosophy professor in Kiel since 1879, translated mainly from the Vedas.

The Essence of the Active Word

Register of Names

(* = without naming)
The course participants are set in italics.

Beckh, Hermann	60
Bock, Emil	32
Böhme, Jakob	29
Curtius, Ernst	13
Deußen, Paul	60
Goethe, Johann Wolfgang von	4, 29, 134, 145
Klein, Johannes Werner	60
Klingebeil, Hermann	124
Laplace, Pierre Simon Marquis de	124
Linde, Herrmann	1, 123, 129, 132, 133, 134, 135
Rittelmeyer, Friedrich	1, 15, 30, 33, 123
Ruhtenberg, Wilhelm	61, 117
Stifter, Ursula	41, 125
Steiner, Marie	vii, ix, 30
Steiner, Rudolf	vii. xi, xiii, 7, 12, 25, 26, 27, 28, 29, 30, 31, 32, 33, 60, 123, 124, 125, 139, 140, 145, 146, 149, 151, 152

Works:

Introduction to the 2nd volume of the Kürschner's edition of
[Goethe's Natural Scientific Writings](#) 1887 (GA 1b)

29, 124, 145

Lectures:

December 30 and 31, 1922, in "The Relationship of the Starry World to Man and Man to the Star World. The Spiritual Communion of Mankind" (GA 219). 124

July 11, 1923, in "The Human Soul in its Connection with Divine-Spiritual Individualities" (GA 224) 18, 124

March 3, 1923, in "Anthroposophical Community Building"
(GA 257) 20, 124
"History of the Anthroposophical Society" (GA 259) 26, 124
June 29, 1923, in "Our Dead" (GA 261) 123
June 8, 1923, in " The Artistic in its World Mission" (GA 276)
41, 125
"An Anthroposophical Foundation for Christian Renewal"
(GA 342) 139

Weber, Friedrich Wilhelm 3, 123
Wohlbold, Hans 30, 124

Appendix I

Speech at the Cremation of Hermann Linde

Basel, June 29, 1923

Dear mourning community!

Our dear friend was one of the first to join our spiritual community in heartfelt intimacy. We got to know his dear, good heart, be it in such an effectively accomplished duty of work, sacred to us all, be it in walking side by side in the confession of our spiritual knowledge, we got to know this good, dear heart. We learned to appreciate it and should know how to remain connected with him, even after our physical eye can no longer look into his physical eye. So, in future, our soul's eye, remembering him with much warmth and love, will look into his dear spiritual eye.

The Essence of the Active Word

The gentle beat of your soul's wings
Carried you, dear friend, in spiritual paths,
Your fate's earnest guiding hand
Brought the spiritual word to your ancestor.

Many a doubt came your way,
But the heart's strength, it found
Through the light of life and the shadow of existence
To the thought goal in the spirit land.

And so look, faithful friend soul,
In the full spiritual reality,
What you sensibly envisioned
As the future after earthly time.

And in the evening of your life you still had to
Deep within the soul our great pain
From the flame terribly shining;
For earthly existence it broke your heart.

Your wife's earnest love of heart,
She will follow your spiritual life;
Your daughter's faithful memory
Shall preserve your noble striving.

And we, spiritually united to you in being on earth,
We who accompany you to the new life,
Want to dwell with you spiritually united
In times to come and in worlds to come.

— — — — — — —

Appendix I

Deiner Seele sanfter Flügelschlag
Trug Dich, lieber Freund, in Geistesbahnen,
Deines Schicksals ernste Führerhand
Bracht' das Geistes-Wort zu Deinem Ahnen.

Mancher Zweifel trat in Deinen Weg,
Doch des Herzens Kraft, sie fand
Sich durch Lebenslicht und Daseins-Schatten
Zum Gedankenziel im Geistesland.

Und so schaue, treue Freundesseele,
In der vollen Geisteswirklichkeit,
Was Dir sinnvoll leuchtend vorgeschwebt
Als die Zukunft nach der Erdenzeit.

Und am Lebensabend noch mußtest Du
Tief im Seelen-Innern unsern großen Schmerz
Aus der Flamme furchtbar leuchten sehn;
Für das Erdendasein brach es Dir das Herz.

Deiner Gattin ernste Herzensliebe,
Sie wird folgen Deinem Geistesleben;
Deiner Tochter treu Gedenken
Soll bewahren Dein edles Streben.

Und wir, Dir geistverbunden im Erdensein,
Wir, die wir zum neuen Leben Dich geleiten,
Wollen geistgeeint bei Dir verweilen
In Zukunftzeiten und in Weltenweiten.

The Essence of the Active Word

Dear mourning community! Our dear friend was one of the first to join our spiritual community in heartfelt intimacy. We got to know his dear, good heart, be it in such an effectively accomplished duty of work, sacred to us all, be it in walking side by side in the confession of our spiritual knowledge, we got to know this good, dear heart. We learned to appreciate it and should know how to remain connected with him, even after our physical eye can no longer look into his physical eye. So, in future, our soul's eye, remembering him with much warmth and love, will look into his dear spiritual eye.

Dear friends! On his serious path of spiritual research, Hermann Linde found many a doubt, many a soul obstacle along the way. He possessed a spiritually inclined soul-a warm inner strength of heart. It led him with strong inner power to what he then found as his spiritual word, his spiritual knowledge, in which we were connected with him in intimate friendship.

One could say that Hermann Linde faithfully followed three epochs of anthroposophical life. First, he discovered this spiritual life. Now occasions arose when he was one of the most effective, the most devoted and the most willing to make sacrifices in Munich, working on our Festival Mystery Plays, which was also his work in collaboration with others. About how many things, my dear friends, we have to admit: in the time we had for working on it, it would not have come about without Hermann Linde.

When the call came to build the Goetheanum on the Dornach hill, which is so dear to us all and which has also died, he was again one of the first to advise and help, offering everything he had to the work — his art and his being. We have seen how Hermann Linde, who had grown out of his life's artistic activity, ultimately sacrificed all that he was able to give in art to the work with which he had completely connected himself.

Appendix I

Anyone who is able to appreciate and love human loyalty and devotion could not help but appreciate and admire the quiet, gentle and yet so energetic a soul working and living within Hermann Linde and feel that he was the dearest soul of a friend who had accompanied us on our spiritual path.

Many of the hours in which I met Hermann Linde working, working beside his dear wife, our friend, up in the dome of the Goetheanum, and in which he sacrificed his best to the work whose downfall he and we had to experience in such deep pain, come before my soul's eye.

When you saw Hermann Linde working quietly in his studio, completely devoted to the Goethe idea, everything he could feel as an artist, secretly immersed in this Goetheanism, then you knew: this was one of the best artists working among us.

Dear mourning friends, this is how Hermann Linde stands before us. However, we also had to accompany him in such a way that we always saw in him how a strong, yearning soul lived in a weak body. For all of us, this weak body took Hermann Linde away from us early, far too early: this weak body, of which those who were more intimately connected with Hermann Linde knew that all the obstacles in Hermann Linde's life, all the doubts that arose in him, which sometimes prevented the intentions of the work from coming to full fruition, came from him. Those who were intimately close to Hermann Linde knew that his soul was great and that he himself often felt an inner tragedy due to his weak body.

Precisely for this reason, his place was in a spiritual community that was able to look beyond everything that only physical-earthly sensuality gives, that is able to look up to that which the spiritually willing soul longs for and hopes for as its great goal as supernatural ability. In intimate friendship with Hermann Linde, the thought often occurred to me: If you may say to yourself that you do not succeed in everything you want in your earthly existence, you may take comfort in the fact that in spiritual regions your will, which wants to transcend the earthly, is strengthened and strengthened and that you are able to give to the earth all that you would like to give it. — Yet we had to say to ourselves: We must not make such demands as Hermann Linde made of himself. — We were truly always in full agreement with this soul, who worked in such a mild, quiet way. We appreciated what he did for us as one of the best.

Hermann Linde can be a role model for many, my dear mourners. He struggled in his quiet inner being, struggled with serious strength and with solemn dignity he persevered beyond all doubt, beyond all inhibitions, to that realization which brings man the certainty that what you live on earth comes from divine heights of existence. — Hermann Linde knew how to appreciate the holiness of the divine heights of existence. Hermann Linde knew how to see through what secrets these divine heights of existence held, and he therefore knew how little of what we bring into this existence from heavenly heights through earthly birth enters into the human consciousness of earthly existence.

It is true that we are all born of God for earthly life. During this earthly life the scant human consciousness is deprived of being imbued with divine power. Only in death experienced with earthly consciousness can the divine power find again the strong soul power that feels connected with the impulse of Christ, and can give birth again, can let the God in the human breast resurrect the connection with Christ.

This too, Hermann Linde felt. Just as he knew that he had been led from God's existence into earthly existence, so he knew that in earthly death lives the Awakener, Christ, with whom the human soul, the human heart, can unite.

Today in this serious hour, we look up with you, beloved soul, into spiritual regions, knowing that the one who preserves the consciousness of divine derivation in earthly existence, who conquers for earthly consciousness the permeation with the Christ-power, will be reawakened, will rise again in bright, light spiritual heights. There, dear soul of a friend, that is where our eyes of friends longingly guide you from the deepest depths of our hearts. We want to let our best thoughts, which were connected with you, follow you there. We know you in the future in spiritual heights. It will be up to us to search again and again from the deepest feelings of our hearts for the thoughts that go to you, that may unite with your aimed thoughts in bright spiritual heights, that want to remain with you for all times, that you will have to walk through for all world expanses that you weave through. Yes, may our thoughts be with your thoughts, out of the earthly work which we could feel, with which you were spiritually connected to us through your own choice in this earthly life.

May your thoughts, my dear mourners, always follow the spirit-bound one into his future earthly, joyful stages of existence, full of light, preparing for a new earthly existence. So let it happen. Now may our thoughts follow you, may they stay with you, our dear Hermann Linde, and may we know how to stay with you, even if our souls have to search for you in bright spiritual heights.

The Essence of the Active Word

The gentle beat of your soul's wings
Carried you, dear friend, in spiritual paths,
Your fate's earnest guiding hand
Brought the spiritual word to your ancestor.

Many a doubt came your way,
But the heart's strength, it found
Through the light of life and the shadow of existence
To the thought goal in the spirit land.

And so look, faithful friend soul,
In the full spiritual reality,
What you sensibly envisioned
As the future after earthly time.

And in the evening of your life you still had to
Deep within the soul our great pain
From the flame terribly shining;
For earthly existence it broke your heart.

Your wife's earnest love of heart,
She will follow your spiritual life;
Your daughter's faithful memory
Shall preserve your noble striving.

And we, spiritually united to you in being on earth,
We who accompany you to the new life,
Want to dwell with you spiritually united
In times to come and in worlds to come.

― ― ― ― ― ― ― ―

Appendix I

Deiner Seele sanfter Flügelschlag
Trug Dich, lieber Freund, in Geistesbahnen,
Deines Schicksals ernste Führerhand
Bracht' das Geistes-Wort zu Deinem Ahnen.

Mancher Zweifel trat in Deinen Weg,
Doch des Herzens Kraft, sie fand
Sich durch Lebenslicht und Daseins-Schatten
Zum Gedankenziel im Geistesland.

Und so schaue, treue Freundesseele,
In der vollen Geisteswirklichkeit,
Was Dir sinnvoll leuchtend vorgeschwebt
Als die Zukunft nach der Erdenzeit.

Und am Lebensabend noch mußtest Du
Tief im Seelen-Innern unsern großen Schmerz
Aus der Flamme furchtbar leuchten sehn;
Für das Erdendasein brach es Dir das Herz.

Deiner Gattin ernste Herzensliebe,
Sie wird folgen Deinem Geistesleben;
Deiner Tochter treu Gedenken
Soll bewahren Dein edles Streben.

Und wir, Dir geistverbunden im Erdensein,
Wir, die wir zum neuen Leben Dich geleiten,
Wollen geistgeeint bei Dir verweilen
In Zukunftzeiten und in Weltenweiten.

The Essence of the Active Word

Appendix II
A Note From GA 342
About This Edition

Regarding the textual basis: The print is based on Karl Lehofer's stenographic transcript. As Lehofer's transcription of his shorthand notes has a number of shortcomings, a certain amount of editing of the text was necessary. The following remarks are intended to provide information on this.

Necessary Remarks on the Quality of the Transcripts

Between the living spoken word of Rudolf Steiner and the printed text are people, people who listened to the lectures with active interest and who wrote down what they heard with very different skills and also with different levels of understanding. When preparing a lecture text for printing, these differences must be taken into account. Before deciding to make any changes, no matter how small, to the text transmitted by the stenographer, editors must try to subtly understand the possible errors that can occur during shorthand transcription or transcription from the shorthand. This includes knowledge of the various shorthand systems and experience in dealing with the idiosyncrasies of the various stenographers.

Shorthand — and this applies to all systems — is a predominantly symbolic script in which there are only characters for the consonants, while the vowels are represented symbolically, for example by superscripts or subscripts of the consonant characters, by close or wide connections, etc. Writing is purely phonetic, without regard to spelling or capitalization.

The Essence of the Active Word

Words that sound the same therefore look the same (example: Meer — mehr; Mal — Mahl). A shorthand transcript can therefore not simply be read, but must be interpreted. It is not enough to know a shorthand system in order to take notes of speeches; you also need to master an extensive abbreviation system (debate writing), a large amount of manual practice, knowledge of the subject matter being discussed and its terminology and, last but not least, a good constitution in order to be able to take notes for long periods without becoming fatigued. Just as ordinary handwriting becomes more volatile and therefore more difficult to read when writing quickly, so it is with shorthand; when writing quickly, the individual stenographic characters can become distorted: Corners round off, tight connections become wide, etc., and this can lead to misinterpretations when transcribing. The various shorthand systems (Gabelsberger, Stolze-Schrey), which were also used by the listeners of Rudolf Steiner's lectures, do not differ fundamentally from each other, but only in the different meanings of the consonant signs, the symbolic vowel representations or the abbreviations. There is no better or worse system; each has its advantages or weaknesses. What can easily lead to a transcription error in one system due to deformation of the characters can, under certain circumstances, provide clearly recognizable written images in another system, and vice versa. The following is an attempt to let the reader participate a little in the editor's work. The work begins by checking which text documents are available for a lecture. If there are no original stenograms, the most important document is the very first, still uncorrected raw transcription by the stenographer himself. It is often possible to see from the shorthand or the first transcription where the stenographer has not kept up or has not been able to read his writing, which special expressions (e.g. unfamiliar foreign words) have caused him difficulties, where quotations have only been noted in passing when taking notes,

Appendix II

with the intention of inserting them when transcribing, and so on. Punctuation, which is not written down but added during transcription, can also be better assessed in this way. In some texts, errors have only crept in during later "corrections", which are then often no longer recognizable as such. Example:

wrong transcription:	... a book on numbers by Ibn Resch
later "Correction":	Ibn Roschd
correct:	Ibn Ezra

The lectures and discussions of this course were co-stenographed by Karl Lehofer — then aged 24 — an employee of the Scientific Research Institute of the "Kommender Tag". Lehofer was a good and conscientious stenographer, but he was partly overtaxed by the tasks assigned to him here. On the one hand, his stenographic skills were only sufficient as long as the speaker spoke slowly; on the other hand, he was not given enough time and peace and quiet to transcribe his shorthand. Ernst Uehli had hired several typists especially for the transcription, to whom Lehofer had to dictate into the machine. Immediately after this raw text was produced, the transcripts were sent to some of the course participants without Lehofer having had the opportunity to work through the raw transcription again using the shorthand and to check any unclear passages.

The present edition is based on this uncorrected first transmission by Lehofer. The private print of the Christian Community from 1978 was only used for comparison. In preparing the text for printing, particular attention was paid to the special weaknesses of Lehofer's stenographic skills, insofar as these are known or can be reconstructed. Unfortunately, no original stenograms have survived, which made this work very difficult.

Errors can already occur when taking notes (omissions, unclear characters, hearing errors), others only occur when transcribing (illegible passages, incorrect transcription of similar-looking characters, incorrect insertion of punctuation, etc.). The following defects or shortcomings occur relatively frequently, especially in texts co-written by Lehofer:

- Omission of individual words or parts of sentences

- excessive shortening of whole words or word endings, which leads to ambiguities when translating. Examples:

    anschau — -en, -ung, -ungen kul — -t, -tur, -tus, -tisch

    Pf – Pfarrer or Professor (pastor or professor)

- Not writing out the verb forms. Example:

    ha   - habe, hatte, hätte, haben, hatten, hätten

    ha — have, had, would have, have, had, would have

- Writing the words heard in the wrong order or in an arbitrary order (= word salad; occurs when the writer does not write immediately while speaking, but rather schematically by ear seconds later). Example:

Shorthand:

The pedagogy and didactics of the Waldorf school always emerge from the entire understanding of anthroposophical life.

Rearranged:

The pedagogy and didactics of the Waldorf school always emerge from the anthroposophical understanding of the whole of life.

When editing the text for printing, minor errors due to

shorthand were carefully corrected. Minor omissions, also due to shorthand, such as omitted articles and slurs, have been added and jumbled sentence fragments have been put in the correct order. Names or quotations incorrectly reproduced by the stenographer out of ignorance have been corrected. In some places where incomprehensible sentences remained due to omissions by the stenographer, additions by the editors were necessary; these additions are indicated by [square brackets]. Where necessary, explanations of the relevant passages have been included in the notes.

No editorial editing in the sense of stylistic smoothing of the text was undertaken, nor was any attempt made to change the particular character of the spoken word. Only where it was necessary for the understanding of the content were sentence changes made.

The punctuation and paragraphs, some of which were apparently inserted arbitrarily when dictating from the shorthand into the typewriter, as is understandable in a raw transcription, were corrected accordingly.

The Essence of the Active Word

ABOUT THE LECTURER

Rudolf Steiner

During the last two decades of the nineteenth century the Austrian-born Rudolf Steiner (1861-1925) became a respected and well-published scientific, literary, and philosophical scholar, particularly known for his work on Goethe's scientific writings. After the turn of the century, he began to develop his earlier philosophical principles into an approach to methodical research of psychological and spiritual phenomena. His multi-faceted genius has led to innovative and holistic approaches in medicine, science, education (Waldorf schools), special education, philosophy, religion, economics, agriculture, (Bio-Dynamic method), architecture, drama, the new art of eurythmy, and other fields. In 1924 he founded the General Anthroposophical Society, which today has branches throughout the world.

This is the guy who designed the Goetheanum, the Father of Organic Architecture! And he did some other pretty creative stuff, also. One of them was to catalogue all of Johann Wolfgang von Goethe's scientific writings — he wrote extensively on this. Steiner authored 28 Books and gave over 6,700 lectures. Our mission is to get the over 3,000 lectures that have never been translated into English, translated into English!

Rudolf Steiner [1861-1925] was an Austrian philosopher and esoteric scientist who, among other things, wrote 28 books, gave over 6,750 lectures, wrote hundreds of articles, essays, verses, and meditations, originated Waldorf Education, Biodynamic Agriculture, Eurythmy, or Art as visible speech, and developed the Camphill Movement to help the aging and those suffering from mental incapacities. The original works were published in German, and as of October of 2022, there were 3,033 lectures that were never translated into English!

About the Translator
Hanna von Maltitz

Hanna the translator and Hanna the artist are successfully combined in this book and others (see "Other Books," below). Her paintings enhance the covers of the books and her understanding of the subjects she translates enhances the interior texts. Hanna's enthusiasm for this work is evident in the quality of her translations. For the translation of this book. she consulted with Priests of the Christian Community to ensure her clear understanding of the material. Her translation work is sponsored by the Basil Gibaud Memorial Trust.

Hanna lives in Cape Town, South Africa. By 2018 she has had 13 solo exhibitions of her yearly 23 paintings at the Novalis Ubuntu Centre. Her portfolio can be accessed on https://www.behance.net/HannaVonMaltitz and you can admire her artistry at the *Fine Art Presentations* site.

THE ESSENCE OF THE ACTIVE WORD

On-line Resources

- Rudolf Steiner e.Lib. *Healthy Thinking*, Bn/GA# 335, translated by Hanna von Maltitz.
- Rudolf Steiner e.Lib. *Der Weg zu gesundern Denken un die Lebenslage des Gegenwartsmenschen*, GA# 335, original German.
- Rudolf Steiner e.Lib. *Healthy Thinking*, Bn/GA# 335, Side-by-Side Compare.
- Fine Art Presentations – e.Gallery. *Hanna von Maltitz* (see more of Hanna's paintings)
- Rudolf Steiner e.Lib:
  https://rudolfsteinerelib.org/
- Rudolf Steiner on Social Issues:
  https://go.elib.com/SocialIssues
- Toward a Threefold Society:
  https://go.elib.com/ThreefoldSociety
- Renewal of the Social Organism:
  https://go.elib.com/SocialOrganism
- The Inner Aspect of the Social Question:
  https://go.elib.com/InnerAspect
- The Social Question:
  https://go.elib.com/SocialQuestion

These on-line resources are wonderful for research … and buying the book to read and study at home is even better! It not only enhances your understanding, but it also helps our being able to continue providing Steiner's never before translated into English offerings. Pass it on!

The Essence of the Active Word

OTHER BOOKS
translated by Hanna von Maltitz

HEALTHY THINKING

(by Rudolf Steiner, translated by Hanna von Maltitz)**:**

This Rudolf Steiner quote from the public lecture of June 10, 1920, in Stuttgart, sums up the essence of these lectures: "We are thinking of a renewal of the whole scientific and spiritual worldview of the present and into the near future." These ten lectures were translated from the original German by Hanna von Maltitz who also did the front Cover Illustration. This is an English First Edition volume in keeping with our promise to print the "not found in English translation" books to a "research on-line and study at home" condition.

Thanks to the *Basil Gibaud Memorial Trust*, this translation has been made available for everyone. The text of both the printed and eBook editions has numerous links to on-line web content that will enhance the reader/researcher in their understanding of the text.

ISBN: 978-1948302371

THE FOUNDATION COURSE

(by Rudolf Steiner, translated by Hanna von Maltitz)**:**

This is a First Edition English translation of a series of eighteen lectures. In this course, *The Foundation Course*, where over one hundred people interested in the questions of a renewal of religious life and activity attended, Rudolf Steiner speaks about the ways in which, through spirit knowledge, religious activity can be fertilized and led into new forms of cultural organization. This text includes the reproductions of blackboard drawings and inscriptions, notebook entries, etc., in-line with the text. It is subtitled, *Spiritual discernment, Religious feeling, Sacramental action*. Thanks to the *Basil Gibaud Memorial Trust*, this translation has been made available for everyone.

ISBN: 978-1948302371

THE IMPULSE OF RENEWAL FOR CULTURE AND SCIENCE

(by Rudolf Steiner, translated by Hanna von Maltitz):

This is a First Edition English translation of a series of seven lectures, entitled *The Impulse of Renewal for Culture and Science*, and published in German as, *Erneuerungs-Impuls für Kultur und Wissenschaft* (Bn/GA/CW Number 81 in the Bibliographical Survey, 1961). Thanks to the *Basil Gibaud Memorial Trust*, this translation has been made available for everyone.

This course was organized by the Federation of Anthroposophical University Work and the Berlin Branch of the Anthroposophical Society.

ISBN: 978-1948302043

THE SOCIAL QUESTION

(by Rudolf Steiner, translated by Hanna von Maltitz):

This book is a First Edition, never before translated into English, series of six lectures. Rudolf Steiner gave these lectures early in the year of 1919 at Zurich, Switzerland. Here Steiner proffers ideas to solve the social problems and necessities required by life, by studying the life sciences and social life, and the living conditions of the present-day humans. Thanks to the *Basil Gibaud Memorial Trust*, this translation has been made available for everyone.

ISBN: 978-1791660536

www.ingramcontent.com/pod-product-compliance
Lightning Source LLC
Chambersburg PA
CBHW070143080526
44586CB00015B/1817